Arnold, Schwinn & Co.

Introduces Super Balloon Tire Bicycles

MODEL B10E

LOW PRESSURE
18 to 22 Lbs.
According to weight of rider

The only major development since the coaster brake—on the finest specially constructed bicycles built by the oldest and most outstanding American manufacturer. A 2⅛″ automobile type double-tube, straight-side, cord tire—on a new deep drop center rim—a construction embodying all the latest advancements in the tire art.

ARNOLD, SCHWINN & CO.
1718 NORTH KILDARE AVE.
CHICAGO,   ILLINOIS
TELEPHONE BELMONT 6793

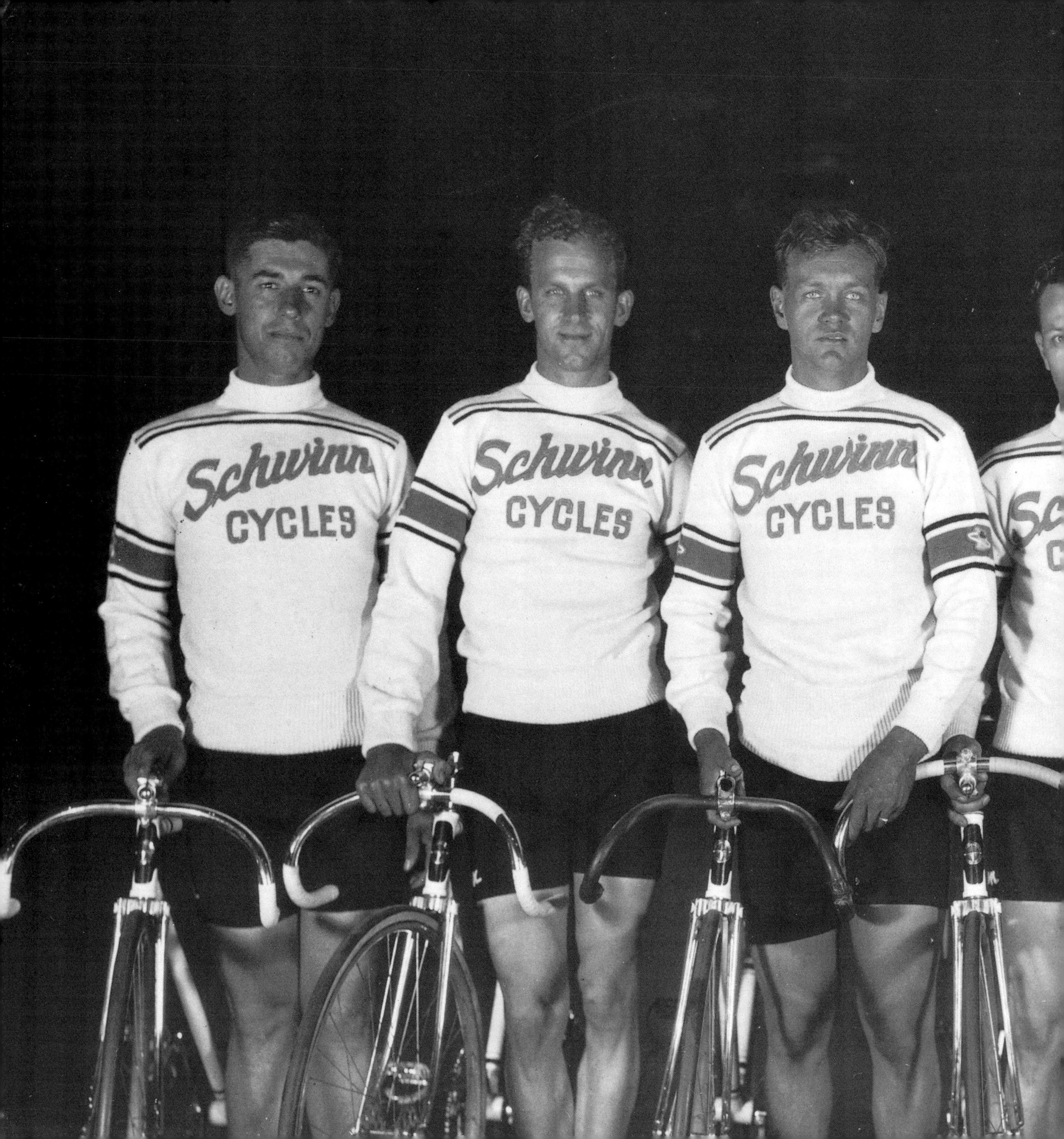
Schwinn
CYCLES
Schwinn
CYCLES
Schwinn
CYCLES

Schwinn
Bicycles

Jay Pridmore and Jim Hurd

MBI Publishing Company

First published in 2001 by MBI Publishing Company, Galtier Plaza, Suite 200, 380 Jackson Street, St. Paul, MN 55101-3885 USA

MBI Publishing Company books are also available at discounts in bulk quantity for industrial or sales-promotional use. For details write to Special Sales Manager at Motorbooks International Wholesalers & Distributors, Galtier Plaza, Suite 200, 380 Jackson Street, St. Paul, MN 55101-3885 USA.

Library of Congress Cataloging-in-Publication Data Available

ISBN: 0-7603-1298-2

On the front cover: By 1959 the Mark IV Jaguar had become "America's Middleweight Masterpiece" with three-speed gears, hand brakes, headlight, and two carriers. Red, blue, green, and black were available.

On the frontispiece: The B10E of 1933 was the original Schwinn balloon-tire bicycle. The durable ballooners were a Schwinn mainstay for years.

On the title page: In the late 1930s, Frank W. Schwinn assembled a crack team of six-day racers, shown here in their team jerseys. Six-day racing was fast-paced, exciting, and very popular.

On the back cover: Top: 1968-1973 Krate series. The design was ingenious. The forward lean of the Krate resembled drag racers, and the smaller wheel enabled engineers to use old tooling for the spring fork that had gone on old Phantoms. The stick shift caused some safety concerns, but that was nothing for young riders who braved the streets of suburban neighborhoods and the dirt on vacant lots. The Krate became a national icon and remains one of the great classic bikes of its era.

Bottom:The 1950 Panther had all the most desirable Schwinn features, like a spring fork and ample chrome, but lacked the cantilever frame. Though the Panther's streamlined lines were considered racy and ultramodern, according to the brochures, true connoisseurs knew that your parents had to spend a bit more for the ultimate, which was, of course, the Black Phantom.

Printed in Hong Kong

CONTENTS

ACKNOWLEDGMENTS

In reconstructing the history of an American institution—which the Schwinn bicycle certainly is—we have tapped many sources. Research and the search for photographs began at the Bicycle Museum of America in Chicago, which was founded in 1993 as the successor to an outgrowth of the Schwinn Bicycle Museum.

The Schwinn Museum was a testament to the company's interest in and respect for the history of the American bicycle. Today, the Bicycle Museum of America provides for all bicycle enthusiasts—and anyone with an interest in popular history—a profound service by collecting and making available to the public evidence of a fascinating aspect of America's industrial revolution.

The authors owe a debt primarily to the Schwinn family. Richard Schwinn, the great grandson of Ignaz, and Peter Davis, Richard's brother-in-law, have been cooperative and enthusiastic in building the Museum. In the process of assembling this book and our previous book, *The American Bicycle*. John Roberts, president of the Museum and publisher of *The American Bicyclist* magazine, has also assisted immeasurably and patiently.

While writing a book of this sort requires quiet sifting through papers, publications, old photos, and other materials, it also depends upon conversations with people who lived through important episodes at the bicycle's past. Interviews with many such people have been critical in our attempts to bring alive the story of the Schwinn bicycle and the people who built them.

Former Schwinn employees who spoke to us and whose contributions were indispensable included Al Fritz, Ray Burch, Frank Brilando, Rudy Schwinn, Bill Chambers, Bill Jacoby, Dolly Becker, Phil Cicchino, Tony Panzica, Dave Staub, Dave Karneboge, Rick Podsiadlik, Charlie Hewett, Ray Caparros, Mike Ferrell, and Jack Smith.

The lives of many other bicycle people were touched by the Schwinn story, and many shared their memories and recollections with us. Jerry Rod-man was a six-day racer on the Schwinn team that was organized in 1938. James Grady, Wes Pinchot, Charlie Churchill, and Larry Bush are now middle-aged enthusiasts who collect either old balloon-tire bicycles or photos that evoke the marvelous sentiments connected to the sturdy and elegant bikes that were icons of the era. Phyllis Harmon, a long-time member and officer of the League of American Wheelmen, was also generous with her time and recollections.

The Schwinn motorcycle story constitutes an important episode in the history of Schwinn, and it is known very well to collectors Richard Winger, Bruce Linsday, and Richard Schultz, and by Jim Rogers of the Motorcycle Heritage Museum in Westerville, Ohio. From the Motorcycle Museum also came photos of the Excelsiors and Hendersons, images which may make the heart of any motorcycle enthusiast race just a bit faster.

Another important part of the Schwinn story revolves around the advent of BMX, told in vivid detail by Russ Okawa, once a young motorcycle mechanic at Canyon Cyclery in Woodland Hills, California. Okawa worked with some of the earliest stars of the BMX circuit and later took the Schwinn factory team on the road.

The mountain bike story was related by some of the pioneers of the sport: Gary Fisher, Charlie Kelly, Joe Breeze, and Wende Cragge among them. Carole Bauer of the Mountain Bike Hall of Fame in Crested Butte helped with the Colorado angle of the history of early mountain bikes. And Ed Zink, owner of Mountain Bike Specialists (aka The Outdoorsman) in Durango, Colorado, and manager John Glover were helpful in telling how mountain bikes developed in their part of the Rockies.

Other folks in Schwinn dealerships were generous in telling us their stories, including Oscar Wastyn, Jr., of Oscar Wastyn Cycles in Chicago, Illinois; Jimmy Hoyt of the Richardson Bike Mart near Dallas, Texas; Jay Wolff of Helen's Cycles in Santa Monica, California; Dennis Hostetler of Glen Ellyn Schwinn in Illinois. Also helpful was Les Bohm of Catalyst Communication, a marketing group located in Boulder, Colorado.

A number of people with the new Schwinn, now called Schwinn Cycling & Fitness were wonderful in describing the successful transition of the company. Mark Schroeder, Skip Hess, and Greg Bagni were enthusiastic about Schwinn history and demonstrated that the new company takes the traditions of the now 101-year old Schwinn very seriously indeed.

Perhaps most important was the indispensable work on this book done by employees and volunteers of the Bicycle Museum of America. Besides President John Roberts were Pam Trammell, Esperanza Llamas, Ben Low, Anna Roberts, and Jonathan Shabica all of whom provided assistance at critical times. Their enthusiasm and goodwill were indispensable. They performed innumerable services on behalf of the authors and for anyone else who finds this book a useful and enjoyable excursion through a rich slice of American history.

—*Jay Pridmore, Chicago*

The Popular Schwinn Hornet...

"It's a Schwinn for me... I've compared them all and for my money, Schwinn's the best!"

INTRODUCTION

Arnold, Schwinn & Company was founded in 1895 in Chicago, just as the "bicycle boom" of the Gay 90s was at its peak. In the few years that followed, many of the hundreds of companies that made fortunes building and selling bicycles went out of business. But not Arnold, Schwinn and its founder, a tough-minded German immigrant name Ignaz Schwinn. The manufacturer's Teutonic tenacity enabled his company to survive the bicycle market's many low points, until the 1930s when America's interest in bicycles surged and sales skyrocketed. Sales booms came again after World War II and yet again in the late 1960s.

Bike booms, when they came, were important in making the Schwinn firm dominant and its name one of the most famous in the United States. Indeed, whole generations of American kids grew up riding Black Phantoms, Varsitys, and Fastbacks or wishing they were. Yet Arnold, Schwinn's real strength was not just in riding over the good times; it was the way it got through the rough spots as well. Indeed, Schwinn prospered so well in the good times because it survived very well through the bad.

The first two decades of the 20th century were hardly flush for most American bicycle makers, as the automobile had replaced the "wheel" in the affections of the American imagination. Yet Schwinn persisted, building bicycles for chain stores and other retailers—at paper-thin margins, to be sure—but keeping the Chicago factory running and growing. Meanwhile, Ignaz Schwinn used his talent for cycle building in the manufacture of motorcycles—Excelsiors and Hendersons—which had their own profitable days in the sun and certainly helped keep the bicycle business going in its darkest hours.

In 1931, the Excelsior motorcycle company was abandoned, Ignaz retired, and his son Frank W. endeavored to bring the bicycle back to the forefront of American life. This he did by conceiving the balloon-tire bicycle—heavier and far more durable than most previous models. For the first time children were encouraged in great numbers to be bicycle riders. The balloon-tire era lasted through the 1950s and helped Schwinn become the most prominent bicycle maker in America by far. While Schwinn had

competitors, and some surpassed the Chicago commune in volume, none matched the prestige of Schwinn nor the quality that Frank W. demanded and backed up with a lifetime guarantee.

Not everything Schwinn did was a rousing success. In 1937, Frank W. set the wheels in motion to build what he hoped would be the greatest racing bicycle in the world, and the Paramount laid fair claim to that title. The problem was that the price tag for a chrome-moly lug-frame bicycle with components of the best possible quality was out of reach for most. Moreover, the idea of adults on touring bicycles—as they were in great numbers in Europe—was slow to catch on in car-crazy America. While Paramounts made a huge impact on the sport of six-day racing in the few years left before World War II, Paramounts remained the best idea that Frank W. ever had that never made a dime, at least in his lifetime.

Schwinn got through the war, though primarily as a weapons supplier rather than a bicycle manufacturer. These years were critical for the company, as the factory, including many women skilled at brazing frames, remained up and running and ready take advantage of the great economic boom that followed the war's end.

As baby boomers became bicycle riders, Schwinn strengthened its position, not just because Frank W. Schwinn's company knew how to design and build very good bicycles, but also because it knew how to sell them. In the postwar years, the Schwinn Authorized Dealer network became the envy of nearly every other company in America for its loyalty, its knowledge, and its almost constant communication with the decision makers in Chicago.

There were rough spots to come, however. In the 1970s, Schwinn was a burdened giant and feeling the strains of age. Its manufacturing methods—notably the once-preeminent flash-welding technique—became largely obsolete as lightweight lug-framed bicycles from foreign countries rose to the top of the market. Schwinn's dealer network, moreover, was expensive to maintain in a period when new bicycle companies in BMX and mountain bikes succeeded through "guerrilla" marketing—showing up at races, making fast impressions on bicycle journals, and taking chances on dazzling new products.

Schwinn's hardest times came in the late 1980s and early 1990s when the company went bankrupt and was purchased by a new group that moved the entire operation from Chicago to Boulder, Colorado. It was not a bright moment for anyone involved. Old-time employees were mostly separated from what had been a true family company. The new owners wondered if they would ever recover from the doldrums of a company in distress.

They did, of course, and are now succeeding on the shoulders of values that were established early on—unimpeachable quality, constant innovation, and utter pride in a name that is still synonymous with the American bicycle. The new Schwinn overcame fresh challenges by virtue of old values and reestablished itself as the most enviable name in American cycling.

Where does Schwinn go as it embarks on its second 100 years? Will it develop increasingly remarkable mountain bikes? Will they continue to enchant the adult market with high-tech revivals of balloon-tire klunkers? Does their future lie elsewhere?

The answer may lie hidden in this history, a history which recently spawned the slogan "legendary innovation" in the offices, design rooms, and factories of the new Schwinn. The people who have inherited Schwinn understand this stuff, and their respect for Ignaz Schwinn, Frank W., and their legions of colleagues appears as genuine as their visions of future bicycles are ambitions.

Left
Ignaz Schwinn immigrated to Chicago in 1891, started Arnold, Schwinn & Co. in 1895, and by the 1930s handed the beginnings of a true American institution to his son Frank.

Above
Frank W. Schwinn, a brilliant engineer, took over the company when his hard-working father retired. Frank W. made Schwinn the most famous bicycle name in America.

Chapter One

THE ORIGINS OF SCHWINN

*E*ighteen ninety-one was the year that Ignaz Schwinn, whose name would grace the most famous head tag in American bicycles, immigrated to the United States. Young Ignaz was unknown when he arrived in America, but he remained confident that his ambition and skill as a mechanic would serve him well in his new country. A place where speed, mobility, and innovation were valued, bicycles had become a thriving industry that attracted the leading technical minds of the day.

Schwinn was born in 1860 in Hardheim, Germany, a remote farming village that remained in the shadow of the industrial revolution. For several generations, his family had been keeping livestock and growing grain on the rolling terrain of the province of North Baden. The Schwinn clan prospered modestly in Hardheim, especially when father Schwinn left the farm and became an artisan piano maker. Nevertheless, there were seven brothers and sisters in the family, and it was natural for Ignaz to set his sights on a different and more independent life.

He attended technical school as a youngster, then apprenticed himself to a machinist where he gained practical knowledge of metals and industrial tools common in workshops. This training allowed young Schwinn to see the world beyond his village and its environs. He began to look toward larger towns and cities—not only in Germany but all over Europe—where new industries and factories were increasing in size and number.

Indeed, growing industries and new factories gave young men like Ignaz Schwinn choices that rural German boys had never even imagined a generation before. He might have chosen to enter the manufacture of iron carriages, gunsmithing, or any of a range of other industries then in the throes of modernization. A clever boy, Ignaz considered the many options open to him. Early in his life, however, it seems that he set his sights on an invention that had intrigued blacksmiths, machinists, and a few far-sighted industrial men for some time: the bicycle.

In the 1870s, however, two-wheelers remained rather clumsy devices. Most bicycles at this time were neither dashing to own nor profitable to manufacture—they were heavy, expensive, and distinctly unsafe to ride. Yet the velocipede, developed and named in France a decade before, looked like a fascinating invention, both to the agile and wealthy young men who could afford such a novelty, and especially to curious young mechanics who saw in the bicycle a basic design to be improved and made available to ever larger numbers of people.

By 1875, Europe's best bicycles were coming out of England where several firms had devised high-wheel models and were exporting a few of them to the continent as well as America. Credit for these handmade forebears to the modern bicycle industry goes primarily to James Starley, a mechanical genius who gradually converted a sewing machine factory, where he had begun as foreman, to the manufacture of Europe's next great technological

Left
In late 1893, Ignaz Schwinn was part of a group that organized the International Manufacturing Company which built and sold a high-grade cycle called the American. Schwinn was a mechanic par excellence who also understood marketing. To promote the American, the company hired a well-known, if unlikely, Chicago cyclist named Baby Bliss.

Above
In the 1890s heyday of racing, *Bearings* magazine printed color portraits—suitable for framing—of the era's great racers such as John S. Johnson, sprint star of the World Team. Ignaz Schwinn and the rest of the world discovered Johnson at the International Championship meet that took place in Chicago during the World's Columbian Exposition of 1893.

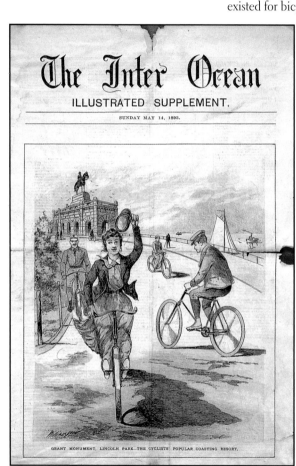

advance. In a model called the Ariel, the Smith & Starley firm of Coventry had made a high wheeler of such quality that it inspired other English mechanics—many also from sewing machine mills and skilled with metal lathes and welding—to enter a new industry that looked very promising indeed.

As the invention crossed the channel and drew notice in Germany, it was natural for energetic journeymen like Ignaz Schwinn to seek work in shops where the proprietor might be dabbling in bicycle designs and even turning out a few of them for sale. After several such positions, Schwinn came to believe that a larger market existed for bicycles, but he also knew that many improvements would be needed before that future could be realized. While Starley was advertising his Ariel as the "lightest, strongest, safest, easiest, cheapest . . ." cycle on the market, Ignaz Schwinn noted that it could, and very likely would, become lighter, stronger, and safer still.

For most of the 1880s, the bicycle business remained intriguing but small, dominated by the high wheeler, a machine with cranks and pedals attached directly to the front axle. This was a simple design but one with a limited following. Primarily, the efficiency of riding such a conveyance owed to the size of the drive wheel, which in some models grew to a diameter size as large as 60 inches or more. While this concept created an elegant and stately machine, it had significant shortcomings, only some of which could be corrected through refinements of the basic concept.

Maintaining rigidity in such a large wheel, for example, was problematic. Starley addressed this difficulty with some success by developing the "tangential" system—spokes attached not radially to the hub but on a tangent so that forward pressure on the pedals tightened the spokes and strengthened the wheel. Tangential spokes enhanced performance and increased sales of high-wheel bicycles. Starley's placement of a step on the frame for mounting was another deceptively simple improvement in the interests of popularity. His development of the hand brake, the first reliable mechanism for stopping the bicycle on command, was a critical development as well.

Still, the market was limited to agile and brave souls who dared to climb aboard a wheel as high as a man was tall (at this time, cycling was almost entirely a male pastime). This, combined with the inherent instability of a high wheeler, made the risk of performing a "header" (an involuntary flight over the handlebars) a dangerous likelihood.

Then in 1884, John Starley, James Starley's nephew, developed what is now considered the original "safety bicycle." The Rover, as this model was called, consisted of two wheels of approximately the same size, cranks hung on the frame with a sprocket, and a chain connected to the rear axle. This configuration kept the rider in a stable position and close to the ground. Proper gearing made it an efficient ride as well. The Rover, though hardly a faultless machine, still stands as one of the important turning points in bicycle design. And while many others quickly took to making improvements, John Starley's original geometry and mechanics were not radically different from what would become the standard bicycle for the next 100 years.

Young Schwinn, Enthusiastic and True

Back in Germany, young Ignaz Schwinn saw the safety bicycle and in it, he believed, the future. In his spare time he drew his own versions of the basic design, and as Schwinn worked in a number of bicycle shops in the next few years, he attempted to interest his employers in the idea of manufacturing such a machine. Mostly, they declined. The high wheeler was still tricky to ride, but it remained a proven thing. Gradual improvements, most makers preferred to believe, would slowly widen the market.

Finally, Schwinn found a factory owner who took his designs for a safety bicycle to heart. The owner was Heinrich Kleyer, of the Kleyer Bicycle Works in Frankfurt, a relatively short train trip from Hardheim. Kleyer was impressed with Schwinn and hired him. Though the Kleyer Works did not convert to the safety bicycle at once, the project gradually developed. By 1887, when the company turned the corner from high wheelers to safeties, Schwinn was general manager of the factory.

Ignaz Schwinn was never a great original inventor, neither in his youthful years nor later for his own company. But he had a distinct talent for noticing good ideas, refining them, and putting them into practice. For Kleyer, he turned out one of the first diamond frames in Germany, and Kleyer's Adler line quickly became one of German's best-known bicycles.

Diamond frames did not end Schwinn's drive to innovate. Many other improvements needed to be made in the machine, and Schwinn continued to read the bicycle literature, test-ride the competition, and discuss problems with other people in the cycling industry. Among scores of potential improvements, for example, was the need for a rear axle that would allow the cranks—and the rider's legs—to remain stationary while the wheels continued to turn by momentum. Schwinn family lore has it that Ignaz was working on such a device in Germany—it became the coaster brake when it was finally perfected some years later in England.

However close Schwinn came to manufacturing a coaster brake in Germany, he certainly realized that his prospects at the Frankfurt factory were limited. The young man was making important changes at the Kleyer Works, but he was unlikely ever to rise higher than plant manager for his employer. Thus, an impulse to immigrate to America crossed his mind—a common course among many young Europeans at that time. Schwinn came to his fateful decision while visiting relatives in the northern port city of Hamburg in 1891. There, as he watched the many ships departing for new and exciting places, his fate was sealed.

Leaving Germany would not happen precipitously. Schwinn discussed the move with Herr Kleyer, and though the proprietor was not anxious for his plant manager to resign, he agreed to write a letter of recommendation. This letter was highly complimentary, calling Schwinn an "enthusiastic" and "true" employee. "I can only recommend him," Kleyer wrote in German. "He does not need help in running a factory."

A Contentious New Industry

When Ignaz Schwinn arrived in America, he found, as expected, many opportunities in the bicycle industry. Here, as in Europe, the industry was on the verge of a great boom. The safety bicycle was bringing many more riders to cycling than the high wheeler ever could. Women, in the early throes of the liberation movement, took to wearing bloomers and "wheeling," as the pastime was called, in great numbers. Clubs grew, and cycling was insinuated in nearly every aspect of American life—even theological debates as some preachers believed it was an evil way to spend a Sunday, and others endorsed it as something divine.

The result was that hundreds of companies large and small became involved in the manufacture of bicycles and associated accessories. Most made claims to significant and indispensable improvements, many in the name of health. The risk, for example, of an apparent Victorian malady called "nerve death" motivated a variety of new saddle designs and also speeded the acceptance of a new innovation from England: pneumatic tires.

The American market was growing rapidly, but it was also stormy and unforgiving. The biggest and oldest player in the bicycle trade of the day, Colonel Albert A. Pope of the Pope Manufacturing Company, proved that it took a hard man to build a smooth-riding bicycle. Pope was the greatest mass-production czar of his day. Even European makers had to admit that bicycles from Pope's large factory possessed "comfort and practical usefulness," as a British journalist wrote in the respected periodical *Scientific American* in 1895, "though some parts hurt our aesthetic feelings, and we would almost call them rather heavy."

Pope's career in the industry began when he was already a wealthy factory owner in the 1870s with interests in the shoe industry and gunsmithing. Always in search of new products, the Colonel traveled with a group of fellow Boston businessmen to the 1876 Centennial Exposition in Philadelphia to witness what new industrial inventions were on the horizon. Among the hundreds of exhibits visited, he became intrigued by a relatively small display of English high-wheel bicycles. He could not get them out of his mind.

Though few agreed with him at the time, Pope believed that bicycles represented an enormous opportunity for any manufacturer who took the invention in hand. He overcame discouragement from almost all of his friends—most said the contraption was too dangerous—and produced a marketable high wheeler. The cycles weren't cheap (they cost several hundred dollars at the time), but cycling instantly became fashionable, especially in Pope's own Boston. Within a few years, the Colonel took over a sewing machine factory in Hartford and converted it to bicycle making.

Pope was more than a factory man. He played all the angles to promote his new enterprise. In his early bicycle-making years, for example, he hatched an ingenious scheme to buy a relatively obscure patent for the basic velocipede. The patent had been granted some years before to a French immigrant named Lallement and was owned at this time by two carriage makers, one in Boston and the other in Vermont. Pope succeeded in buying the patent through a scheme in which he was almost in both places at the same time. The story is that he snapped up the Boston half of the patent rather easily, partly because its owner believed he could always get the other

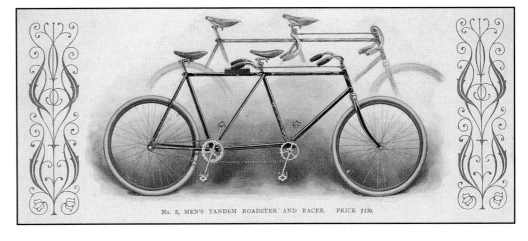

One of the earliest bicycle makers in Chicago was Gormully & Jeffery, innovators in frames, tires, and other aspects of the cycle. G & J also owned the name Rambler, which Thomas Jeffery retained when he left the bicycle business at the turn of the century to enter the entirely new automobile industry. This illustration from the 1897 catalogue shows the No. 3 Combination Tandem.

No. 3, MEN'S TANDEM ROADSTER AND RACER.   PRICE $130.

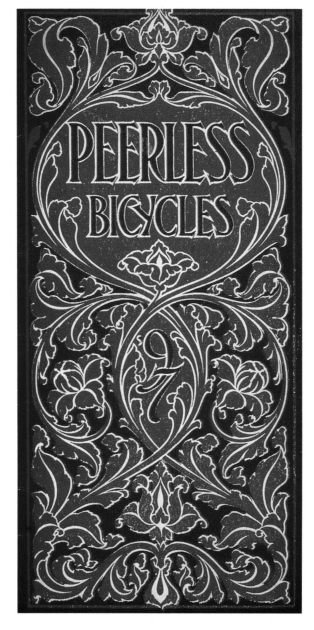

labor, many of them complicated and peculiar to this art; whilst in the same machines many different tools are often used and are supplemented by the use of scores of hand and bench tools . . . ." Having perfected the art of precision machining, Pope's factory was one of the earliest true mass-production plants anywhere. "This one large American factory is larger than any three across the Atlantic," continued *Leslie's*.

Pope met his match in few people, but Albert Overman, owner of Overman Wheel Works, was one. Overman got his start some years after Pope but developed a business that led the industry in the bicycle's heyday. Overman's genius, like Pope's, was in efficient manufacturing—so much so that *Scientific American* described the Overman factory in Chicopee Falls, Massachusetts, as one of the most efficient in the world. "Nothing but a huge machine itself," the magazine declared in 1891.

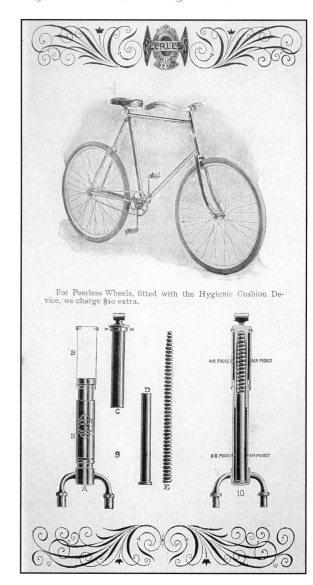

For Peerless Wheels, fitted with the Hygienic Cushion Device, we charge $10 extra.

half if he needed it. But before the first carriage maker could get a message to his partner in Vermont, Pope was on the midnight train. By morning he was full owner of rights, he believed, to any vehicle with two wheels, cranks, and pedals. Pope began demanding fees from all bicycle makers in the United States, mostly in New England and New York, and he got them.

The Lallement patent was to expire in 1883, and safety bicycles were soon to displace high wheelers. But Pope's energy and inventiveness had just begun. His bicycle plant in Hartford was one of the most modern of America's industrial revolution. In 1882, *Leslie's Popular Monthly* marveled at Pope's operation in near-lyrical terms: "158 different machines perform their automatic

Overman had "the utmost regard for system," and the bicycles he turned out, called Victors, were generally regarded as equal or superior to Pope's Columbias.

As the boom years of the 1890s drew near, Pope and Overman were its true aristocrats. But the nature of the bicycle trade in this country was hardly genteel. Competition grew fierce, even personal. Early on, the primary arena for the two barons of bicycling to fight it out was in the patent office and in the courts. Litigation over rights and licenses became routine news in the industry.

Detachable pedals, "hygienic" saddles, methods for compressing rubber onto a rim—these were among the endless innovations battled over in court. While many smaller makers bowed to Pope's aggressive position in patent matters, Overman went nose to nose with his competitor. He even hired a former governor of Connecticut to represent him in court. Tens of thousands of dollars were spent, amazing sums to the smaller makers who continued to work on innovations of their own and hoped only to avoid the kind of patent battles that could easily bankrupt them.

Meanwhile, even the careful legal positions of Pope and Overman did nothing to stanch the flow of dollars from both of their coffers. The situation reached a peak in 1886 when Pope and Overman concluded the "Treaty of Springfield," a pact made when the two met at the national championship cycle races in western Massachusetts that year. "It was termed an honorable settlement," wrote *Bicycling World* magazine. Still, it did nothing to dampen the competitive spirit of these quiet but relentless entrepreneurs. As the safety bicycle was accepted as the next step in the American bicycle's evolution, Overman, Pope, and a number of others competed tooth and nail for that business—a battle that was now focused in the designing rooms and advertising offices. (The courts would not grow overly quiet, however.)

In 1887, Pope introduced his version of the safety bicycle, the Columbia Light Roadster, which had modest suspension and hard rubber tires. By 1889, Overman came out with his, the Victor Model A. The Victor foreshadowed diamond-frame geometry; it also included an elaborate spring front fork assembly (anticipating soon-to-be standard design), and still-experimental pneumatic tires.

Overman appeared to have an edge with his Victor safety and began buying lavish advertisements stating in no uncertain terms that this model deserved to be considered the finest bicycle in America. Pope, making improvements of his own in the meantime, tolerated the ads only as long as it took for him to place one of his own and announce a challenge: The Pope Manufacturing Company had deposited $1,000 with the editors of *Bicycling World*. If Overman would do the same, a panel of judges would be selected to determine the superior product.

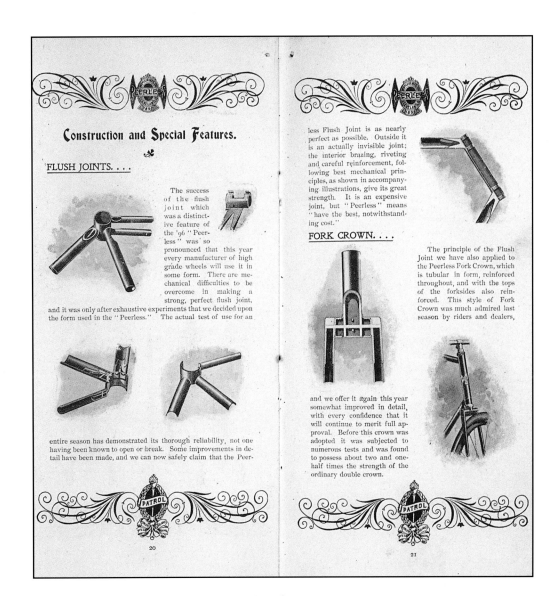

Overman at first ignored the dare, and bicycle pundits seemed to agree that Pope had the better of this publicity skirmish. That was until one of Pope's advertising men slipped. Perhaps it was overconfidence—at any rate he placed an ad with a reproduction of an allegedly Chinese scroll, purporting to be an ardent testimonial to the quality of the Columbia safety bicycle. This would have been impressive, but only if it were true.

Overman's people, suspecting a ruse, noisily put up their $1,000 for anyone who could provide a direct translation of the so-called "Chinese letter." An interpreter came forward, and *Bicycling World* printed what the Overman publicity office presumably had discerned on their own. The Chinese characters were utter gibberish.

"It is meaningless," said the translator. "Some of the characters can hardly be recognized as Chinese. It looks like Japanese-Chinese and a vain attempt at copying the original." Overman had revenge.

of patent-office volume, and a separate section was established in Washington for the industry alone.

Chicago and the World's Fair

Clearly, Ignaz Schwinn was entering an expanding, if raucous, business environment when he arrived in the United States in 1891. Little is known of his voyage to America or who met him when he arrived. It was clear all along, however, that Chicago was his destination. Indeed, Chicago's name rang with new opportunity. It was the gateway to America's migration west, the young nation's railroad hub, and a magnet for new industry. Hundreds of thousands of people were migrating to Chicago every year, and its future seemed as unlimited as the people's collective ambition.

Schwinn's choice of settling in Chicago may have had another more specific cause. In 1890, the city had been chosen as the site of the nation's next great world's fair. Much was expected of the World's Columbian Exposition, scheduled for 1893. It would house, promoters promised, the most remarkable displays of technology that the world had ever seen. It would feature palatial architecture, the world's first Ferris Wheel (constructed, it was said, like a giant bicycle wheel), and electric lighting to illuminate the grounds and buildings with unimaginable intensity. Nothing could keep Chicago from hosting the biggest and best world's fair ever.

Nor could anything keep the bicycle manufacturers at the fair from making a good showing of themselves, despite the fact that exposition officials had relegated them to the mezzanine level of the Transportation Building. While railroads, carriage makers, and related industries got prime space, the bicycle builders made a loud protest of their poor location, studded the building with signage to attract sightseers, and even engaged a brass band to lure traffic upstairs.

Once there, the showgoers found lavish bicycle exhibits. Canopies, bunting, and fringe decorated the booths along with the latest models from scores of manufacturers competing in the business at the time. While bicycles were fairly standard at the time, many exhibitors tried mightily to attract attention. Gendron Iron Works, for example, had a painting of a nude cyclist to demonstrate the proper riding position. Since motion and activity could always draw a crowd, another exhibitor had home trainers, with rollers and odometer, and an undersized youngster to race and defeat all comers.

If Chicago was not the biggest bicycle-making city in the country before the World's Fair, it became America's bicycle capital afterward. One of the earliest bicycle concerns of the city was that of Gormully & Jeffery. R. Phillip Gormully was a wealthy tin roofing contractor, and Thomas B. Jeffery was a machinist. Together they

Where Crescent Bicycles are made.

Above and Opposite
Western Wheel Works became one of the largest bicycle makers in the nation, not through any great innovative prowess but because the Chicago-based company had remarkable salesmanship and distribution. Early in his career—before he launched his own company—Ignaz Schwinn ran a factory not far from Western; the lessons of that successful manufacturer and many other makers in Chicago were not lost on the energetic German immigrant.

But it was now the Gay 90s, and the bicycle market was too hot for anyone to be much poorer for it. America had entered the decade of an unabashed bicycle boom. Fierce competition did not always bring out the best in advertising experts, but it was fertile ground for the pure inventor. As the bicycle grew in popularity and as patent litigation was an ever-present threat, bicycle companies kept hard at work on new and original ideas to improve their lines. The numbers alone were staggering. In the United States, 7,573 patents for bicycles and related inventions were on file in the U.S. Patent Office by the end of the 1890s, and it was probably double that throughout the world. Estimates were that bicycles accounted for two-thirds began their foray into bicycles by advertising for capital with a bold guarantee against any losses due to patent infringement suits. By 1883, Gormully & Jeffery were making high wheelers, although their early product literature was less bold on the subject of infringement—they were initially under license to the Pope Manufacturing Company. Happily, the Lallement patent would expire in 1883, and G & J was soon off and running with a growing, competitive business.

Jeffery was a mechanical man of great skill and an innovative turn of mind. Shortly after founding the company, he experimented with one of America's earliest safety bicycles, with cranks and treadles like those then used on sewing machines. By 1888, he had devised a chain-driven model with "a yielding or elastic joint which absorbs nearly all the vibration caused by car tracks or cobblestones," as described in promotional literature. It was called the American Rambler.

Though their safety bicycle would require more time and additional refinements, Gormully & Jeffery quickly emerged as one of Pope's and Overman's major competitors. G & J introduced new saddles and also a "cushion" tire that promised a gentler ride. Later, after Gormully's death—and after the bicycle boom's abrupt end at the turn of the century—Jeffery's vision, as well as his talent for designing new machines, made him a major figure in the next great chapter in American ingenuity: the automobile. Moving to Kenosha, Wisconsin, the Thomas B. Jeffery & Co., later Nash Motors and then American Motors, continued with his famous Rambler trade name.

Another Chicago concern was also growing furiously at this time. This was Western Toy Company, later to become Western Wheel Works, which developed the bicycle business less through mechanical innovation and more through the personal and commercial talent of a former bookkeeper for the firm. R.L. Coleman understood markets, knew retailers, and possessed consummate sales skill. And by the end of the bicycle boom, Western Wheel Works was the nation's highest volume bicycle maker, though far from its most inventive.

Chicago became a magnet for many smaller makers in the trade as well—including Featherstone, Spalding, Hill, and Moffat—along with countless suppliers and retailers. Many of these concerns quickly assembled themselves in and around Chicago's central business district, the Loop, and particularly on a stretch of Wabash Avenue that became known as Bicycle Row. This was one of Schwinn's first stops when he got off the train in Chicago. His first opportunity came a few blocks away from Bicycle Row with the Hill Cycle Manufacturing Company, which hired him primarily on the strength of Herr Kleyer's recommendation.

Kleyer was correct: Schwinn could run a factory, and he soon rose to superintendent of the Hill plant, maker of

A FEW PUNCHING PRESSES.

the well-respected Fowler line. Hill was an ambitious firm at this time and already successful in the then uncommon marketing approach of building stock bicycles in several different sizes. For two years at Hill, Schwinn applied his mechanical and metallurgical knowledge in quest of the industry's holy grail of the 1890s: lighter and faster machines.

Cycling and Social Mobility

Meanwhile, the bicycle was having a profound impact on society in general, and nowhere more strongly than in Chicago. By the 1890s, more than 100 bicycle clubs existed in the city, and some reports had that number

Defiance Bicycles were one of many bicycle makers in the Windy City dedicated to promoting cycling as a polite pastime for civilized and progressive men and women.

up to 500. The bicycle, initially a pastime for the well-heeled, was making inroads into all levels of society that decade. So meteoric was its growth that journalists, who often took an inordinate interest in the new and the strange, began equating the cycling pastime to American democracy itself. It increased mobility for working classes, some claimed. It provided new means for young people to explore outside their neighborhoods and meet, perhaps court, others from different areas and stations in life.

Bicycle clubs themselves also tended to erase social distinctions, as it was common for the rich to enjoy a day's ride along with those from less privileged economic classes. Cycles came to represent freedom, and as the pastime grew, it was natural for politicians to do what they could to connect themselves to the bicycle phenomenon. In Chicago, Carter "Man of the People" Harrison, Jr., was elected Mayor in 1899 partly on the strength of a better-roads campaign, an issue high on the agenda of legions of local wheelmen.

Politically speaking, liberal populists were normally successful among the wheeling crowd, but the explosive

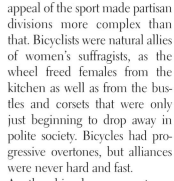

appeal of the sport made partisan divisions more complex than that. Bicyclists were natural allies of women's suffragists, as the wheel freed females from the kitchen as well as from the bustles and corsets that were only just beginning to drop away in polite society. Bicycles had progressive overtones, but alliances were never hard and fast.

Another bicycle proponent was Frances Willard, a suffragist to be sure, but also president of the Women's Christian Temperance Union. Many wheelmen were anything but teetotalers, most enjoying a healthy draft after a good Sunday ride, and instinctively took exception to Willard's views. When the *L.A.W. Bulletin* reviewed her book, *How I Learned to Ride a Bicycle: With Some Reflections Along the Way*, it could not help but point out her "half-concealed sermonettes" with implications about the evils of drink. "Just how she managed to think these noble and perfectly proper thoughts while trying to learn to ride a wheel will puzzle a good many beginners," wrote the reviewer.

So much for politics. Cycling was taking on a life of its own that transcended even the burning issues of the day. It became one of America's most popular sports.

Amateur racing had been in the public eye for some time—ever since the fierce rivalry of high-wheel riders sponsored by Overman and Pope. That was in the mid-1880s when Overman's man George Hendee was "the pet of the whole American world," according to *Bicycling World*, for his brave and noble triumphs in this relatively dangerous sport. In time, W.A. Rowe emerged as Hendee's main competition, riding, not surprising, the Columbia cycle. The public was keenly interested in their matchups, and Rowe finally captured the crown from Hendee in 1886 in an emotion-filled event that left many crowd members weeping in the stands when the race was through.

Racing continued to grow, especially as the safety bicycle allowed higher speeds and more thrilling races. It was an activity to which Ignaz Schwinn paid considerable attention, partly because of the pleasures of sport, but more because racing was an indispensable part of the bicycle business. While amateurism, however shaky, was still upheld throughout most of the bicycling world, victories on the track still constituted the best possible publicity for makers of ever-lighter, ever-faster machines. All serious makers took a keen interest in racing and were rarely adverse to violating rules with discrete payments to racers who rode their machines.

To my old friend Mr Schwinn who builds this bike in 1893

A.D. Kennedy

Morrison

HAYMARKET THEATRE
161 WEST MADISON ST.
CHICAGO.

Track racing was already covered lavishly by the nation's press when a huge meet, including the first-ever world championships, was held in Chicago in August 1893, scheduled during the World's Columbian Exposition. Schwinn managed the riders racing on Fowlers that week, when the best cyclists from Europe, America, and as far away as South Africa met at the 1/3-mile dirt track encircling the South Side Ball Park for one of the biggest bicycling events to date. If Hill-sponsored racers were undistinguished in the field that week (and they were), young Schwinn had an eye for new talent, and there was plenty of it.

Quite naturally, the great Arthur A. Zimmerman was one of the favorites at the Chicago meet, and true to form, Zimmy won a number of early races, primarily sprints in distances up to one mile. Zimmerman, one of America's first truly international sports stars, possessed uncommon pedaling speed—so much so that he usually rode a cycle in a lower gear than most competitors and could perform amazing bursts close to the finish line.

While Zimmy's wins in Chicago may have been predictable, the surprise of the meet was John S. Johnson, a young man from Minneapolis. In the five-mile national championship, in which Zimmerman was once again considered the favorite, Johnson not only demonstrated raw athletic skill, which he certainly had, but also benefited from the kind of teamwork that was being perfected and was winning races.

By setting an unrealistically fast pace, teammates working with Johnson quickly sapped most of the strength from the great Zimmerman before the four-mile mark. They also drafted for Johnson, breaking the atmospheric pressure, as journalists explained in detail, and preserving their lead man as much as possible for the finish. Toward the end, Johnson and Zimmerman were neck and neck and, with less than a lap to go, it looked like Zimmerman would make his customary sprint to the finish and win the race.

But in this case, Johnson was on him, pulled past Zimmy, and crossed the finish line more than a length ahead. The crowd was aghast but also willing to cheer for the young victor. And the race was quietly noted by Ignaz Schwinn, watching from the infield. It not only introduced Schwinn to a great young racer—their paths would later cross—it also strengthened the German's resolve to satisfy a longtime ambition. That was to start his own bicycle company, sponsor his own team, and surprise everyone by sprinting past established competition.

A.D. Kennedy, one of the top racers of the early safety-bicycle era, went to Hill Cycle Manufacturing and its superintendent, Ignaz Schwinn, for the lightest and fastest bicycle possible. Kennedy later became a member of Schwinn's own World Team.

Chapter Two

"Soaring on with Lightning Speed"

In 1895, the Bicycle Boom was well under way. After more than a decade of experimentation, designers agreed on the diamond frame as accepted standard form—as it would remain for a century. Pneumatic tires were now de rigueur on most models, replacing hard rubber. American industry now manufactured improved steel tubing, which made bicycles lighter and stronger.

Best of all, prices were coming down, with some models under $100—which was considered the barrier to a wider market. The results were rising sales and even grander projections—400,000 bicycles for 1895, some said, up from 250,000 the year before.

Several years of good news lay ahead for the bicycle industry, but already the business was often mixed with caution. Many voiced concern about oversupply, and longtime cycle men cast a wary eye on a flood of new makers in the trade. Most threatening was "cheap goods at high-grade prices," according to one Chicago manufacturer interviewed by the bicycle magazine *Bearings* in its effort to identify dangers in the market ahead.

"Too many barber shops, cigar stores, haberdashers, etc., are selling bicycles, and at figures which stand for but 50 to 60 percent of the list prices of the wheels," complained another maker. "Demoralization" of the business was in the offing—a fact which the *Minneapolis Tribune* frankly and probably inaccurately blamed on the bicycle makers themselves. The paper bluntly challenged manufacturers' customarily high prices. A mass-produced bicycle cost

Baby Bliss & Michael

nowhere near $100 to build and sell, the paper claimed, and current prices were akin to "bank robbery."

Accusations such as these were inflammatory and riled the public, notwithstanding the difference between a truly "high-grade" bicycle and lesser machines for which dealers could and did cut prices. And the question was still burning when *Outing* magazine, another leading cycling journal of the day, printed a rundown on the cost of capital, tooling, salesmen, and (not incidentally for the magazine) advertising to compete in this quickly overheating market.

Other ominous signs for the bicycle market included swindlers aplenty, such as one group calling itself the American League of Cycle Associations, so named to imply a relationship with the leading cycling organization of the time, the League of American Wheelmen. Through a combination of fast talking and fine print, itinerant salesmen convinced gullible buyers to put money down on a bicycle and simultaneously sign up as partners in the company. Many customers not only lost the down payments when their wheels never came, but also were surprised to learn that they were legally liable for the company's mounting debts. Many victims of this scheme were ministers—preachers were beginning to regard Sunday rides on a bicycle as spiritual refreshment and were apparently easy marks.

Stories such as these bloodied legitimate dealers who suffered from the justifiable fear that supply in the bicycle market might soon outstrip

Left
Starting a race at Buffalo, New York, in 1896 were two members of Schwinn's World Team: A.D. Kennedy (third from left) and Johnnie Johnson (third from right).

Above
He was a true bicycle man, but Ignaz Schwinn never let pride stand between himself and a little publicity. He had used the renowned cyclist, Baby Bliss, for publicity in the pre-Arnold, Schwinn days, and later had the 400-pound-plus wonder photographed with his legitimate racing star Jimmy "Midget" Michael.

At the turn of the century, horses shared the oval at Chicago's Garfield Park, but it was the cyclists, on banked turns and with high-speed pace teams, who excited the crowds

Right and Opposite
Shortly after opening Arnold, Schwinn & Co., the proprietors invited the photographers in to document their well-run factory. A decade before, the factories of Pope and Overman had been lauded as state-of-the-art industrial plants, though both older concerns would eventually fail. By the 20th century, Arnold, Schwinn was saying that they were the leaders in volume as well as manufacturing systems.

demand. Thousands of enterprises got into the business in the 1890s, not only driving prices down but also putting out inferior goods as well. In fact, it was easy to ignore troubled aspects of an industry that continued to generate huge increases in revenue every year.

"Medium-grade wheels listed at equitable prices are meeting with a big demand," reported *Bearings* magazine in 1896, an assessment that was more hopeful than precise. "Cheap goods at high grade prices are meeting with extremely poor reception. The public has apparently become tired of being played as the festive sucker in the inflated list confidence game." Beyond the manufacture of low-quality bicycles, several years of planned obsolescence among respectable makers had created an entirely new and troubling segment of the market: the pre-owned bicycle. Used bicycle salesmen quickly established an unenviable reputation for selling damaged goods, and most accounts indicate that it was probably deserved.

The Founding of Arnold, Schwinn & Company

For many reasons, 1895 might have seemed like a poor time to start a new bicycle company. Ignaz Schwinn thought differently. Yes, he would say, sharps and downright crooks existed in the business. And prices were coming down. Yet young Schwinn's concept of the bicycle was basic. A good machine should be strong yet light. It must be sold by knowledgeable dealers. It should be promoted not with mere words but by success in the arena of closest scrutiny: bicycle

racing. Schwinn firmly believed that a bicycle manufacturing concern operating under these conditions
would prosper.

Despite pessimistic rumblings in the industry,
Ignaz Schwinn got his message through to another German in Chicago, Adolph Arnold, a successful meat
packer who was also a partner in a bank not far from
Bicycle Row. Arnold had witnessed firsthand the enormous growth of the cycle business along Wabash
Avenue, and it was natural for a man of his capitalistic
nature to covet a portion of it. Meeting at German social
gatherings, Schwinn discussed with Arnold the details of
building and selling high-grade bicycles. Schwinn's
enthusiasm and obvious experience in the business
erased any doubts the older man might have had.

Thus was born Arnold, Schwinn & Company in
the fall of 1895. With bicycle knowledge coming from
Schwinn and money coming from Arnold—capitalization amounted to $75,000—the firm was established in
a rented factory space at Lake and Peoria streets, west of

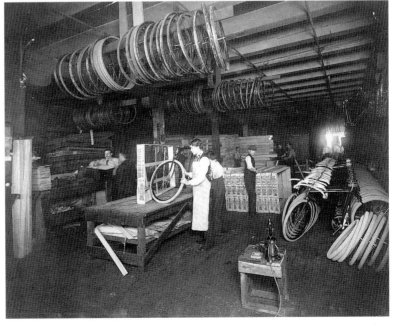

If any cycle merchant missed the point when they were at the trade shows, Arnold, Schwinn & Co. advertising stressed that World cycles were a hit. Why? Because the men who built and sold them were always WIDE AWAKE.

downtown Chicago. The two men were determined to capture the high end of the bicycle trade, which Schwinn assured Arnold was still profitable.

From the beginning, Arnold, Schwinn frames consisted of the best available steel tubing and carefully brazed joints. Ignaz Schwinn also devised a drop-forged one-piece crank, which replaced the usual (more expensive) mechanism of machined parts assembled with pins. Arnold and Schwinn did not ignore talk of a downturn in the industry, but they believed emphatically that excellent manufacturing and aggressive salesmanship they could overcome it.

Almost immediately upon the firm's establishment, Arnold, Schwinn & Co. announced a new and unusually extensive line of cycles. Magazine advertisements announced seven different models, some featuring a selection of frame sizes. The models reflected Schwinn's knowledge of the market and his determination to fill every established niche therein. He was also careful not to tempt fate by following risky new trends, such as the shaft-driven bicycle that so enchanted several major makers at the time. Arnold, Schwinn's standard roadster was an elegant rendition of absolutely standard diamond-frame geometry. It boasted an impressively light weight of 22–23 pounds. A racing model along the same lines tipped the scale at a scant 16–18 pounds, according to a report in *Bearings*.

Schwinn also showed confidence in another American standard: the bicycle built for two. The introductory

line included a Double Diamond tandem and a Combination, the latter with a dropped frame in front for the lady of the house. The Combination was the tandem of choice for Ignaz and his wife, Helen, and they had a child's seat installed between the front seat and the rear handlebars. It was originally for their first child, Frank, born in 1894. Perhaps the most extraordinary bit of engineering from the new company was a racing tandem, spare in design and with the lightest-gauge tubing available. "The weight will be under 32 pounds, which will make it one of the lightest tandems on the market," stated a reported in *Bearings*.

Despite general uneasiness about the state of the market in 1895–96, Arnold, Schwinn & Co. enjoyed a good reputation and steady sales from the moment it opened its doors. This was due largely to Ignaz Schwinn, already well known in Chicago cycling circles, as well as others connected to the firm who instilled confidence. Among Schwinn's colleagues was Edward C. Bode, once one of Chicago's most prominent wheelmen, who had made a name for himself in younger days as a racer on the old Washington Park track. Since that time he had become well-versed in the bicycle trade. He previously worked with Schwinn at the Hill Manufacturing Co., and since then several other companies. Bode's salesmanship was considered expert. "He is a convincing talker and never lets go of a man until he sells him wheels," wrote *Bearings*, a publication for which Bode sold advertising before going to work on the manufacturing side.

In the dynamic bicycle market of the day, Schwinn and Bode believed it was essential to recruit the best possible agents throughout the country to distribute and sell their bicycles. To achieve this, both men spent much of their time in the firm's early months on the road, touting the quality of the Arnold, Schwinn bicycle and the company's ability to produce it. While other manufacturers were doing likewise—and established companies naturally had a leg up—Schwinn and Bode quickly devised a plan to get retailers interested in the new Arnold, Schwinn line. They staged an open contest for the selection of a trade name. The company advertised that a cash prize was waiting for that person who suggested the mark that the firm eventually used.

The winner was the "World," submitted apparently by four separate dealers; each received $100 for its efforts. This name was more descriptive of the company's ambitions than its current prospects, as Arnold, Schwinn, like many U.S. bicycle makers, was anxious to sell its wares abroad. This market simply did not materialize, despite the undeniably high quality of the best American machines of the day, but "World" sounded strong and prestigious, an image that Schwinn and Bode hoped their wheel would soon cultivate.

Words did not substitute for hard work, of course, but words did matter in this business, largely because so many of them were being written and printed in the half-dozen or more cycling publications covering the industry at that time. The fact was that much promotional copy in full-page advertisements was frankly unconvincing, such as poems written in praise of products. "Swift and silent moving steed/Soaring on with lightning speed," was how one cycle was described by a copywriter whose pallid verse may well have been better than the product itself. Arnold, Schwinn & Co., for its part, broke through the advertising drone with a direct and effective appeal to retailers. In its paid ads in early 1896, the company printed in bold type at the bottom of the pages:

"We are hustlers and want hustlers."

Schwinn made ripples in the market and even created a modicum of fear among competitors, such that the new company found it necessary to use a portion of its advertising budget to debunk a rumor. "Jealous competitors and rival bicycle makers state that we can not deliver World Cycles," they wrote. Such rumors, the company declared, were "Lying Statements. . . . We can deliver 1,200 finished machines every month. . . . Send in your orders. We promise to ship at first sight."

While Arnold, Schwinn & Co. developed a network of distributors and retailers on both coasts, it turned out that its best market was in its own backyard. Chicago itself was emerging as the center of the cycling industry, not necessarily because of the hard work of Schwinn and Bode, but the new company certainly enjoyed the benefits. The focus of the bicycle market was shifting west by

The bicycle boom was long gone, but Schwinn continued to turn out high-grade bicycles, particularly for the racing game which still generated international interest. This 1916 World was the one-millionth made by Arnold, Schwinn & Company, in business for 21 years by this time, and one of the leading bicycle makers in the country.

Arnold, Schwinn & Co.

(Incorporated)

The "World" Cycles

240 to 254 West Lake Street

Chicago, U.S.A.

Letterhead for Arnold, Schwinn & Co., circa 1900

There was nothing shoddy or haphazard about Schwinn's manufacturing methods. The enameling department, in this photo taken at the Kildare Avenue factory in 1916, worked in the most orderly and well-lighted conditions.

increments. One measure was the 1896 Chicago Bicycle Show, an exposition that impressed the entire industry for its size and quality. It was followed a few weeks later by the New York show that compared unfavorably. (The important cycling magazines were, admittedly, in Chicago by this time, which may account for a slight bias. Yet the Chicago hall had a new and luxurious amenity, electric lighting, which suggests that in the selling game, the hustlers really were moving west.)

Meanwhile, Arnold, Schwinn & Co., which had hardly shipped anything by the time these two shows opened, was getting high praise by reviewers who stopped by its booths. Undoubtedly, positive press reflected good relations between the firm and the reporters covering the industry—Bode's past connections obviously paid off—but everything about Schwinn's first trade show appearances that year indicated that the company was first-class. A *Bearings* writer, for example, wrote approvingly of a large electrical globe revolving over the Schwinn display in Chicago. There was also friendly and knowledgeable expertise on hand. "E. C. Bode, superintendent of agencies, is ever ready to talk of the merits of World Bicycle. . . principle features expatiated upon were the inside connections, flush joints, one-piece crank and axle, and the tool-steel bearing all through."

There was no doubt that Ignaz Schwinn understood not just the business of the factory floor, but the sometimes notorious aspects of promotion. A year before founding his own company, for example, Schwinn hired a rather unlikely cycling hero named Baby Bliss. This Chicagoan had already developed a reputation as a cyclist of sorts and became the 487-pound mascot of the American line of bicycles, for which young Ignaz was briefly a partner prior to striking out with Arnold. The association figured prominently into a minor episode of Chicago cycling history.

In July, 1895, the rotund rider was chosen to lead the grand march at a "bloomer dance" in Chicago's Jackson Park, a soiree for wheelmen and especially wheelwomen in "rational dress." As bloomers were

perfect for pedaling but still disreputable for polite society, local police were eager to make arrests. The situation led to a prominent report in the next day's newspapers, a fact that did nothing to harm Mr. Bliss's ample reputation, nor that of the 23-pound American that he was paid to ride.

With the World, however, Schwinn revealed a serious side. He remained absent from efforts to identify the next fad in the cycle trade. Indeed, many magazines of the 1890s, including the prestigious *Scientific Ameri-*

can, continued to report on dazzling new technical ideas. Gear-shifting mechanisms were being introduced, though none were graceful enough to catch on. Strange unicycles—one with the pedaler sitting inside the single large wheel—were on drawing boards and some were in production. An aluminum frame also came out in this period, introduced from an unlikely source, the St. Louis Refrigerator & Wooden Gutter Co. Schwinn was uninterested in any untested diversions. World bicycles were built primarily with 20-gauge (1 1/8 inch) steel tubing, the standard on high-grade cycles at that time. Self-confidence and not gimmicks was the company's competitive edge.

The World Team

Ignaz Schwinn did believe in one aspect of the industry that might have been considered a side issue. That was racing, a controversial subject at the time because of differing views and loud debate on the issue of professionalism. While the taciturn Schwinn

Arnold, Schwinn built bicycles on which countless head tags were attached. The reason was that each store wanted its own label, or if not its own then one that was not available down the street. When the Chicago-based makers of Admiral bicycles left the trade early in the century, Arnold, Schwinn was only too happy to have another name to add to its list. This catalogue came out in 1920.

ADMIRAL MODEL NO. 410

The tandem was perfected for racing in the late 1890s, and this multicycle, the "Quint," was designed to pace for the likes of racers "Midget" Michael and Johnnie Johnson on the fastest tracks in the United States. For those who were unimpressed with racing, however, the five seater was also used in road shows like this one at a fair in Grand Rapids, Michigan, in 1897. The globe became the World trademark; riding blind through city streets, happily, was not.

breathed hardly a word on this subject to reporters—who were always in search of copy to fill their magazines—he simply went ahead and put under contract the best pro riders he could find.

Professional racing by no means had the full support of the cycling community at this time. Some still considered it unseemly, that taking money for races was a violation of the amateur's love of sport. No matter that the best "amateurs" routinely traded their prizes of jewelry and even real estate for cash. Through the early 1890s, as the bicycle boom swept across the country, many cycling officials professed outrage that anyone would ride for anything but the privilege to compete.

In the middle of this losing battle was the League of American Wheelmen, formed in 1880 to promote cycling in general and to fight the fight for better roads in particular. The L.A.W.—with a formidable membership of well over 100,000—also became the sanctioning body for racing and remained opposed to professionalism of any sort until 1893. That was when the organization faced the reality of the situation and established a separate category, Class B, for "makers' amateurs," or racers who received financial support from manufacturers.

L.A.W. President George Gideon wrote hopefully that Class B racing was "destined apparently to become the great popular class of the near future. . . . The Class B man, if sufficiently speedy to command a salary from the manufacturer whose wheel he rides, to say nothing for presents made for him for an exceptionally satisfactory win or a broken record, lives on just as much of the fat of the land as suits his digestion."

The fact was that the popularity of cycling in the Gay 90s made the fat of the land very abundant indeed; thus the issue of professionalism was only to grow. Around 1896 there sprung up the National Cycling Association, a professional race circuit outside the jurisdiction of the L.A.W. Purists found this situation beyond the pale and painted the professionals vaguely as outlaws. Some even blamed the powerful but indecisive League. "The toleration of the 'makers' amateur' can be viewed only as a tacit acknowledgment by the L.A.W. of its inability or lack of desire to cope with a troublous situation," read one column in the dignified *Harper's Weekly*. The writer reasoned that the L.A.W. had been seduced, as much of society, by the sensation of track racing as opposed to the "really more valuable and certainly more wholesome field of good roads and general wheeling." But ranting against money was then, as always, a lost cause.

Ignaz Schwinn, who knew the racing game as well as anyone, had little to say in this debate, but his actions spoke for him. He knew that sponsorship of racers sold bicycles, pure and simple. He was moreover opposed to half-measures in any aspect of business. Thus, it was natural for him to envision a well-paid team of racers riding under the World trademark. In 1896, he signed up John S. Johnson, the emerging star from Minneapolis who had been making a name for himself, as well as money on the pro circuit, ever since his surprise win at the world's fair meet in 1893.

Success in racing being fragile, Schwinn preferred not to depend on just one big name in the racing business. Also put under contract was the best-known bicycle race trainer in America, Thomas W. Eck, a silver-haired and intense man whose commitment to winning gained him more victories than it did friends. Indeed, there probably was room for gentlemen in the world of pro racing at this time; Tom Eck was not usually counted among them.

Yet Eck understood better than most that respect in racing came not from good fellowship, but from winning races and setting records. As a result, his determination to succeed was obvious to all who knew him. He often glared at opponents before the start of a race in an attempt to unnerve them. He was not above pulling strings to keep top competition out of races. (One such story concerned the great black racer, Major Taylor, whom Eck attempted to bar from a race, ostensibly because of his color, but more likely because he feared that Taylor might win.) On other occasions, the trainer could become so frustrated that he physically attacked opponents.

Character defects did not stop Schwinn from putting his money on Eck, any more than controversies about pro racing dampened his commitment to hiring the best team he could. Clearly, successful racing would garner notice for the new World line and promote Schwinn's ability to build the best bicycle on the track. Racing, moreover, would help sharpen the skills of his new company—everyone from the engineers whose task it was be to build lighter and faster machines, to publicity people charged with getting the word out when World Team racers collected victories.

Eck shared the same philosophy, and in a long *Bearings* article entitled "The Future of Racing" he expressed his view. "Racing at the present time has virtually become a business," he wrote. "Large prizes have a tendency to create public interest in the races." Eck also insisted that there was no immorality in riding for cash. "A man who spends several years on the racing path and gives up his youth for the amusement of the public should be well paid and have a balance to his credit at the end of his racing career. . . ."

A strange twist was added to Schwinn and Eck's enterprise, however, when they announced that their first serious foray would not take place on the banked tracks of this country. Instead, the World Team would go to Europe and compete with some of the best riders in the world in Paris, London, and other points where cycle racing was a great attraction as well.

There were many possible reasons for this move. One was that the purses, particularly in France, were larger and entirely above board. This appealed to Eck and Johnson, naturally, as did the high level of competition that awaited them. Another advantage of racing in Europe that spring was to gain experience in pace racing, already popular in France and England but unknown in America at the time. Pacing consisted of big, fast multicycles—tandems, triplets, and machines for as many as five and six riders—setting the pace and cutting wind resistance for the racer following on a single. In longer events, a team of several multicycles shared pacing duties, and these races were always exciting with fresh pacers maneuvering on the track to replace spent ones, often at the risk of high-speed disaster.

The World Team sailed for Europe in early March, 1896, an event accompanied by some fanfare. A farewell dinner was given in Minneapolis at John S. Johnson's new house. When Eck spoke at this dinner he noted that "he believed the gathering was the first one ever held in a house purchased with the cycle winnings of the host," as reported by *Bearings*, which also noted that Johnson had paid $7,000 for the fine Victorian home.

Whatever Schwinn and Eck's expectations for the European trip, there were some disappointments. Early on, Johnson had a hard time defeating the class of Europe on their own turf, though he did eventually garner his share of wins and even set a few minor local records. Johnson's trouble, it was reported, was the steepness of the banked turns in Europe. Johnson needed to hit those turns at the precise, strategic instant, and that would take some additional experience, explained Arnold, Schwinn's Edward Bode when quizzed on the subject by a reporter.

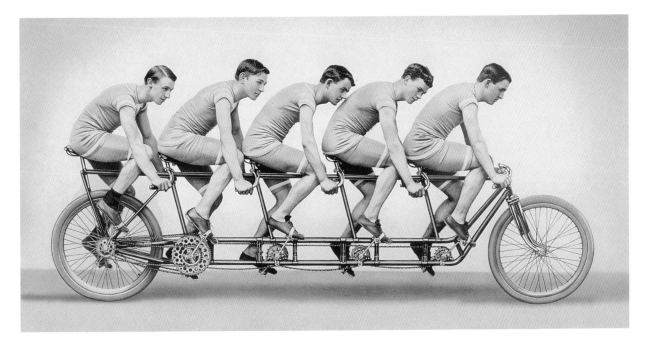

The Schwinn Quintuplet was not the biggest pacing bicycle on the tracks in the late 1890s, but it was one of the best known. Coached by trainer Tom Eck, the pace riders who cut through the atmospheric pressure for more famous racers behind them were nearly as strong and smooth as marquee attractions like "Midget" Michael and Johnnie Johnson.

Multicycles led quite naturally to the bicycle built for two (or three) and the notion that families could enjoy a leisurely ride in the country. Pictured are Mr. and Mrs. Ignaz Schwinn and their son, future Schwinn president, Frank W. Schwinn.

Whatever the truth of this matter, and whatever the real expectations of the World Team, Arnold, Schwinn & Co. was anything but shy in describing the tour in paid advertisements. Full-pages were purchased in the cycling press, emphasizing broken records and continued triumphs. These exaggerations conflicted only somewhat with the news stories that Johnson was having trouble getting wins.

An unexpected benefit of the 1896 European tour came later that season when the team was in England. London was the much-anticipated setting for an encounter between Johnson and the Welsh sensation Jimmy "Midget" Michael, one of the greatest racers of the era. Michael was just over five feet tall, but he had the reflexes of a gazelle and the legs of a workhorse. These traits made him the king of the middle-distance events.

In fact, Eck and company arrived in England at a propitious moment, for Michael was not in the best shape. He had been recently married, a happy state of affairs for him but not for his training regime. He was also carrying on a public feud with his trainer, the well-known "Choppy" Warburton. Thus, the first Johnson-Michael match was an anticlimax with Johnson breezing to a win in the mile race. Later that day, Michael defeated Johnson in the 10-mile distance, though this result was viewed more as a matter of superior pacing than the raw performance of either racer. In fact, Michael seemed to be in a funk.

While Arnold, Schwinn's full-page advertisements broadcast Johnson's win, Eck and Schwinn saw an opportunity in the Michael situation. They convinced him that he should join them on their trip back to America. Professional racing was about to come out in the open at home, they told Midget, and there was plenty of money to be made in the United States.

When Michael finally "crossed the pond," the promise held true. Within a year he was telling curious reporters that he was making $30,000 for some three months work in America. That included guarantees and purses for racing as well as a salary from Schwinn and another sponsor, Morgan & Wright, the Chicago-based maker of pneumatic tires.

One of Michael's early appearances in this country was in the well-known Quill Club Wheelmen's meet on the track at Manhattan Beach in New York City. The crowd of 1,000 was given a great show that day especially in the "hour race," a contest to ride the most miles in that length of time. Michael and American Frank Starbuck were the main competitors, riding behind pacing teams—this being a new twist for the American race fan. "Several multicycles appeared on the track," wrote *Bearings*, "and these three, four, and five-seated machines were also cheered. Nothing like it had been seen in America before."

Clearly, Michael and Eck's experience with multicycles paid dividends as the pacers rode on and off the track with ease. Michael steered smoothly behind each multicycle in turn. Naturally, a bit of Americanism kept the crowd shouting for Starbuck, who almost made up the distance he lost in the rocky early stages of the race. In the end, Michael set an American record of 27 miles, 690 yards in one hour. Many cheers went up, but they were for Starbuck as well, which prompted Frank Fowler, a former colleague of Schwinn's when both worked for the Hill Manufacturing Co., to offer a wager of $1,000 on a rematch. Neither Eck nor Schwinn responded, preferring to bask in the warmth of Midget's victory in New York.

Back in Chicago, cycle racing was about to reach a fevered pitch as well, much to the delight of Ignaz Schwinn. Evidence of great enthusiasm came October 3, 1896, the day Chicago's new cement bicycle track at Garfield Park was dedicated. Eck declared beforehand that the new oval would prove to be the fastest track in the world. On the card that day were several races, but most notable would be serious assaults on major time-trial records by Johnson in the mile and Michael in the five mile.

An amazing 25,000 (some said 40,000) crammed the grounds for the inauguration of the Garfield Park facility, and the police gave up trying to keep them out of the infield. All heard politicians

In the 1890s, the World Flyer had geometry, gearing, and handlebars that were worked out for the best racers in the business.

deliver lavish praise to themselves for building the track, but the crowd was obviously anxious for the riding to begin. Their eyes were not only on the famous racers, but also on the big multicycles, rarely seen in Chicago, warming up slowly around the white cement ribbon. These impressive machines included a World "quintuplet," recently designed and built in Chicago by Arnold, Schwinn.

When the important events finally began, no one was disappointed. Johnson set an American "exhibition" record in his paced mile of 1:40 2/5. In the five-mile event, Michael's smooth pickups of three fresh pacing cycles in succession got him the American record for the five mile with a time of 9:38. The crowd thundered. Both they and the World Team would be back for more, and anyone who missed the events could read about them in the cycling press. Almost wryly, Schwinn's advertising writers listed the new records set on World cycles as their "week's work."

With success, the company was suffering from a bit of hyperbole. The fact of the matter was, however, that Ignaz Schwinn, only five years in this country, contributed mightily to a great cycling center, just as Chicago was having much to do with the creation of the most famous cycling name of the new century to come.

The famous racer Jimmy Michael died while making the trip from Europe to New York on the *Savoie* in 1904—the cause was the effects of a head injury suffered the year before. Sadly, his death was little noted at the time, and he was buried almost without ceremony in New York. In 1949, old-time racing stars along with the Schwinn company joined together to give the once famous cyclist a proper head-stone, donated by Frank W. Schwinn. In the wheelchair is Charlie "Mile-a-Minute" Murphy, the first cyclist to hit 60 miles per hour, paced by a train, in 1899.

Chapter Three

SCHWINN'S MOTORCYCLE ERA

Fear and greed drove the bicycle industry in the latter stages of the Gay 90s as the "bicycle boom" steered itself headlong into the equally dramatic "bicycle bust."

The industry had grown too large too fast and became saddled with capacity of some two million bicycles annually. Even in the best of times, the market was unlikely to absorb so much merchandise year in and year out. The simplest solution to this business problem, and certainly the most ill-advised, was for manufacturers and merchants to continue generating revenue by cutting prices.

These were unhealthy circumstances even without a new bit of engineering on the horizon—the automobile—which would replace the bicycle in the public's imagination with disconcerting speed. Nevertheless, many cycle concerns jumped on the discounting bandwagon with reckless abandon. By 1898, a group of bicycle makers in Toledo, Ohio, announced that they had a contract to produce as many as 45,000 bicycles for a syndicate of department stores including Rothschild's in Chicago and Gimbel's in Philadelphia. Retail prices for these bicycles would go as low as $13.25, and while anyone could sell a store-full of bicycles at that price, the scheme was certain to flood an already flagging market.

Bicycles at this price hurt the industry in another way—the machines were inferior in almost every detail, from the steel in the tubing to the rubber in the tires. Naturally, the buying public at large would ignore the difference between cheap and high-grade bicycles, at least until they got the merchandise

home. Then they would wonder why they had ever bought a bicycle in the first place.

As department stores took out excited advertisements promising low prices, some manufacturers attempted to stem the low-quality tide. One such effort, albeit too little too late, came when the Monarch Cycle Company sued Ludwig Brothers department store for selling a cheap model from the Monarch factory—intended for export only—as the maker's high-grade model. In court, Monarch won the battle, but the industry was losing the war. The flood of substandard merchandise continued to make the bicycle business a cutthroat proposition, and as revenues of once-prosperous companies sank steadily, so did their reputations. Perhaps most distressing to true wheelmen was the bankruptcy of the Overman Wheel Company in 1897. Overman, Col. Pope's first and most worthy competitor in the high-wheel days, had earned a reputation for the most reputable bicycle on the road in the heyday of the bicycle boom.

In an act of desperation, several of the most powerful bicycle magnates of the period attempted to take the bad situation in hand. In 1899, A.G. Spalding, bicycle maker and baseball magnate, installed himself in a rented suite at New York's Waldorf Astoria Hotel and held court before a succession of manufacturers from around the country. Their interest was in forming a large bicycle monopoly, a company that was soon christened the American Bicycle Company or ABC. In fact, Spalding was only the front man in this enterprise,

Ignaz Schwinn was a natural mechanic and entrepreneur, which led him into automotive experiments early in his career. Here driving with his partner Adolph Arnold in the seat beside him, Schwinn built this prototype horseless carriage before the turn of the century. Unlike his Chicago neighbor Thomas Jeffery, who made Rambler bicycles and then cars, Schwinn stayed in the cycle trade, though he was putting motors in them in a few years' time.

capitalization of $80 million was quickly reduced by half. By 1903 the company had defaulted on its bonds.

Independent bicycle makers were cheered by the demise of ABC. Iver Johnson of Fitchburg, Massachusetts, stood as an example. The Iver Johnson Company, which had earlier severed ties with retailers who demanded lower quality and prices, was making some headway in advertising against the would-be monopoly. "Our bicycles are not made by a trust," Iver Johnson's publicity declared.

Predictably, the feisty Ignaz Schwinn had little patience for the Trust, though his advertising during this fragile period was quieter on the subject than that of Iver Johnson. An independent streak in the young German—along with the World's success on the racing track—made Pope's monopolistic ideas completely unacceptable to Schwinn. He had built solid relations with retailers around the country—this would be a long-time Arnold, Schwinn trait—and the still-small Chicago bicycle company would survive if not flourish through these hardest of times for the industry.

Another reason for Arnold, Schwinn & Co. to maintain independence was that Ignaz Schwinn was already looking beyond the confines of muscle-powered conveyances. He and other bicycle entrepreneurs were growing interested in the thing that was clearly fascinating everyone at the time: internal combustion engines. Indeed, there was plenty going on. In 1895, Chicago had hosted the nation's first automobile race, which prompted even the most promotion-minded bicycle journalists to admit that the motor car would soon eclipse the bicycle as the primary object of public affection. By the turn of the century, that was coming true, and it was hardly shocking that two of America's automobile pioneers were previously bicycle men—Frank Duryea and Henry Ford.

No doubt, the skills inherent in bicycle manufacturing were central to the development of motorized vehicles. Roadworthy tires, chain and shaft drives, and even differential gears were first worked out by cycle makers before they were ever incorporated into a commercially viable car. Arnold and Schwinn were hardly blind to the opportunity, and Ignaz was quick to work on the problem. Schwinn's first motorized effort came in 1896—basically a horseless carriage with spoked wheels and a tiller for steering. A succession of three other prototypes culminated with a four-cylinder, water-cooled roadster in 1905. The prototypes never went into production, however. The principals had other things on their mind.

Perhaps it was the bicycle which remained in the blood of Ignaz Schwinn that kept him stubbornly laboring in that business through the worst years of the bicycle bust. "We stand for quality even if the public is not

headed by Col. Pope, still the most powerful man in the industry, who believed that if he could dominate the industry as he once had, he could set it right.

The American Bicycle Company, also known as the "Bicycle Trust," quickly absorbed almost 20 large- and medium-sized manufacturers, but it never came close to a monopoly. While ABC purported to control capacity of 660,000 bicycles yearly, the "independents" credibly claimed that they were producing almost twice that. Which meant that price wars continued and factories closed, all while the public's attention was taken up almost entirely by automobiles and their more affordable relation, motorcycles.

Pope's company had active public relations, as always, which kept the Trust's stock at respectable prices for a while. But the whole enterprise was fraught with so many irregularities that the New York Stock Exchange refused to list the company. More seriously, of course, the obvious oversupply of bicycles led to the inevitable suffocation of the company's finances. Initial

willing to pay for it," he said as bicycle competitors dropped all around him. Steadfastness, of course, would only go so far. Schwinn still had to come up with something new.

The Lure of Internal Combustion

Inventors had started imagining a bicycle with self-contained power almost as soon as men climbed on their first high wheelers. As early as the 1860s, evidence exists of brave wheelmen attempting to attach primitive motors to rickety cycles. Reasonable functionality in such an invention was slow in coming, of course, and most people's response to a hot and noisy steam engine propelling a 60-inch bicycle was much the same as our own might be—entirely too dangerous.

By the 1890s, internal combustion was sufficiently developed for a new set of attempts at the motorcycle. Something that looked like one was promoted by an ambitious entrepreneur named Pennington who introduced his good-looking prototype and showed it off at a number of bicycle shows in 1895. In brief demonstrations, Pennington created a small surge of excitement for what looked like a surprisingly lightweight and efficient motor-driven bicycle.

Pennington accomplished what he had intended, which as it turned out, was little beyond attracting investors. According to *Bicycling World*, "Old Pennington was the first to use electric ignition, and he took advantage of the fact that no one knew much about it to claim that his method of igniting the mixture with electric sparks produced 'refrigerating' action that made cooling unnecessary." The con man collected a few dollars for disreputable efforts and soon disappeared.

By 1898, workable motorcycles were getting built. These were developed initially for the bicycle track by race teams in search of faster and more efficient pacing machines—though one of the first such "motorpace"

races was definitely not a success. Held in Boston in 1899, the event headlined a team organized by bicycle maker Frank Waltham using a gasoline-powered motorcycle in front of the great racer, Major Taylor. Taylor raced well that day, or at least he got off to a good start. But then his opponent's pacing machine, a steam-powered cycle, spewed and sputtered so effusively that the race had to be called off. While the Boston spectators were disappointed—and not a little derisive about it all—the race did represent a turning point. Waltham continued to work on the concept. He soon perfected a one-cylinder four-stroke engine with a 12-pound coil to produce a spark and left the bicycle business altogether to concentrate on the motorcycle.

Ignaz Schwinn, meanwhile, was looking for ways to diversify beyond building and selling bicycles. With his healthy profits from the early Arnold, Schwinn days, he had become involved in real estate with an investment in a luxury apartment building not far from his own house on Chicago's West Side. But like the old

Above and Left
Ignaz Schwinn built a succession of automobiles, such as the Roadster pictured in front of his West Side Chicago home around 1905, and an earlier effort a year or two previously. He eventually decided to leave the technology to other former bicycle men such as the Duryea brothers and Henry Ford, though the Schwinn family always enjoyed fine cars— Ignaz drove a Packard and Frank W. Schwinn, the son pictured in both photos, later drove a Cadillac.

In 1911, just as Ignaz Schwinn and his son Frank were designing and preparing to produce a new motorcycle, the Excelsior Supply Company went bankrupt and was put up for sale. Excelsior sold an array of motors, parts, and most significantly, a popular belt-driven motorcycle. The Schwinns bought the company and in 1913 built this classic, Chicago–style structure for Excelsior which was to become the third-largest motorcycle maker in the United States, after Harley-Davidson and Indian.

Below and Opposite
The Excelsior catalogue from 1916 introduced the factory hands and the well-known racers who helped make "Good Old X" famous. The single-cylinder Lightweight is an interesting cycle for many reasons, not least because of the spring front-fork mechanism that would be a part of the classic balloon-tire bicycle that Schwinn would build two decades later.

mechanic that he was, he remained determined to stay in cycles, somehow, and that would be to build them with motors.

Whatever promise the motorcycle held, Schwinn's partner Adolph Arnold was destined not to be a part of it. Schwinn family lore has it that Arnold was ready to move into motorcycles with Ignaz, but the younger man said he preferred to make this move by himself. Fine, said Arnold, but you're on your own with the bicycle business, too. Though Arnold, Schwinn & Co. built and sold an estimated 50,000 bicycles in 1907, margins were paper-thin and profits were nearly nonexistent. Arnold obviously considered bicycles a liability. So, happy with

his own small slice of the now-past bicycle boom, he bid his former partner good-bye and good luck.

Great Names in Motorcycles

Like anything that Ignaz Schwinn did, he embarked on the motorcycle business with tenacity and cut no corners. Shortly after parting with Arnold, he had his engineers design what might have been, if it had been built, a motorcycle to overshadow anything else being made at that time. It featured vertical twin cylinders and a driveshaft—this while the market was dominated by single cylinders and leather belts. Detailed plans left behind show that Schwinn was ready to revolutionize the industry. (Vertical twins did not catch on until the late 1930s when England's Triumph began to mass produce the design.) "Schwinn engineers had gotten to the point of designing fasteners and estimating piston velocities for the new machine," a writer for *American Motorcyclist* magazine wrote after discovering and studying these unused drawings years later in 1995. It was "remarkably advanced for its era."

But Ignaz Schwinn chose another direction. Instead of building a new Schwinn motorcycle, he continued to investigate and study the industry. He attended shows and examined products that would compete with his own. Then in 1911, Schwinn and his brilliant son Frank were informed that the Excelsior Supply Company, with a Chicago warehouse and factory not far from Schwinn's own, was bankrupt and being run by a

Men Who Have Helped Make The Excelsior Famous

Here are a few of the racing men who have pinned their faith to the Good Old X and have thereby gained in money and reputation.
Carl Goudy won the American National Championship at Chicago, September 12, 1915, and of the five world's speed records established last year, four went to Carl Goudy and the Good Old X. Not only that, he won every race held during 1915 in which a new World's Record was established.
Bob Perry won his title "King of the Dirt Tracks" on an "X", and in spite of many brilliant inducements, has stuck to the machine that Always Makes Good.
Joe Wolters is another man who has attained fame and affluence on the X.
Glen Stokes, the California wonder, holds a number of World's Records and National Championships, all won on the X.
Lorenzo Boido and C. A. Hillard are later additions to the Excelsior team; but are already making good.
Wells Bennett is an endurance rider who has won more perfect scores than any other man on the Pacific Coast and was one of the two Excelsior riders who won perfect scores in the Los Angeles Endurance Run of 987 miles in three days, in which only four men were able to finish.
The above are by no means the only riders who have participated in the building of the Excelsior reputation, but space forbids showing them all.
Lee Humiston, the only man who has ever officially attained a speed of 100 miles per hour, established that record on an X, together with World's Records for many other distances, one to 100 miles, that have never been equalled in spite of strenuous efforts to do so.

Service Department

No matter how good a motorcycle may be, accidents, and in the course of time natural wear and tear, call for replacements and in some instances repairs that can be properly accomplished only at the factory.
To meet these requirements, the service department is maintained under the supervision of Arthur G. Lyon, a man who worked on the first Excelsior Autocycle ever built and has always borne an important part in connection with their production.

Excelsior dealers and thousands of riders have learned that in case of disaster, their port of refuge is Art Lyon who knows exactly what they need and sees to it that they get it at the earliest possible moment.

A. G. LYON

committee of creditors. Excelsior was a large supplier of parts for engines of all kinds, and several years before had begun manufacturing motorcycles.

This was Schwinn's chance, which he took by purchasing Excelsior's entire business for $500,000—the sale included the building, all inventory, and $200,000 in back orders. It was an advantageous acquisition, to be sure, and it represented a running start for Schwinn in the motorcycle business. While there were as many as 100 other companies making lightweight single-cylinder models at this time, Schwinn was able to distinguish itself quickly.

Fortunately, the motorcycle industry was about to enter a boom not too different from the bicycle-boom years of the 1890s, and Excelsior (as Schwinn's motorcycle company was still called) was poised to take advantage of it. Ignaz Schwinn and his company quickly mastered many aspects of building and selling motorcycles. Frames, for example, entailed a heavier version of the brazed bicycle frame that Schwinn had been making all his life. He also had in-house engineers, led by his precocious young son Frank, who were ambitious and excited about staying on top of developments in a growing market. Several years later, for example, Ignaz and Frank were very nearly ready to offer a new four-cylinder, shaft-drive motorcycle, the equal to anything else then on the market. Though it was designed, it was never produced. Their detailed drawings showed that the Schwinn family was as adept at motorcycle innovation as they were in bicycles.

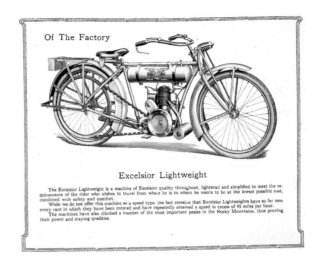

Of The Factory

Excelsior Lightweight

The Excelsior Lightweight is a machine of Excelsior quality throughout, lightened and simplified to meet the requirements of the rider who wishes to travel from where he is to where he wants to be at the lowest possible cost, combined with safety and comfort.
While we do not offer this machine as a speed type, the fact remains that Excelsior Lightweights have so far won every race in which they have been entered and have repeatedly attained a speed in excess of 45 miles per hour.
The machines have also climbed a number of the most important peaks in the Rocky Mountains, thus proving their power and staying qualities.

Once again, another opportunity intervened. The Henderson Motorcycle Company of Detroit was foundering, and its owners were looking for a buyer. It was an attractive opportunity because Henderson was one of the best big bike manufacturers of the era. Its problem was that owners Tom and Will Henderson, entrepreneur-sons of an executive of the Winton Motors Company, could not cope with the materials shortages and price increases caused by World War I.

Schwinn purchased the Henderson company in 1917 with hopes that a sleek four-cylinder machine might compete with the enormous expansion of the automobile industry occurring at the same time.

A Trip Through The EXCELSIOR Factory.

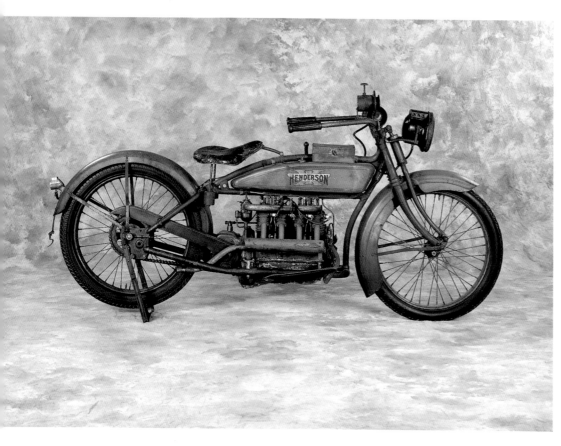

1918 Henderson. At the end of 1917, the Schwinn family bought out the Henderson Motorcycle Company of Detroit and moved the operation to Chicago. Henderson was one of the premier four-cylinder motorcycles at the time. The Schwinns put extra heft in the prior Henderson frame design but otherwise maintained the Henderson's reputation as one of the most elegant motorcycles ever built.

The 1919 Excelsior Series 19 was the line's "military version," devised when the company produced machines for the American and allied military during World War I. An Excelsior motorcycle like this 61-cubic inch, side-valve V-twin was the first to make 100 miles per hour in 1913.

Schwinn's terms for the Henderson company were generous, and they included jobs for the brothers: Tom in sales and Will in engineering.

The acquisition had a happy outcome for a while. The Henderson was merged with the Excelsior line, and the Schwinn-owned company became the third-largest maker of motorcycles in the country, after Harley-Davidson and Indian. And as the market expanded, the company managed to get past several rough spots in the road. Two of them were the Henderson brothers themselves, whose personal relationships with the Schwinns were not destined to last. Will in particular was dismayed by changes in the Henderson Four—he believed it was too heavy and sacrificed speed. Tom also believed that the Henderson, always considered one of the most elegant motorcycles on the market, was taking a more utilitarian and market-oriented direction. Sadly for Ignaz, they soon left the company.

Other of Schwinn's hopes for the industry turned out to be unrealistic—one was that the U.S. Army, about to enter World War I, would establish a motorcycle division along the lines of other motorized divisions. Excelsiors saw wartime service, mostly for couriers speeding to and from the front, but a mounted battle division would have raised demand for motorcycles by 40,000 per year, Schwinn estimated, with Excelsior supplying a significant portion of it.

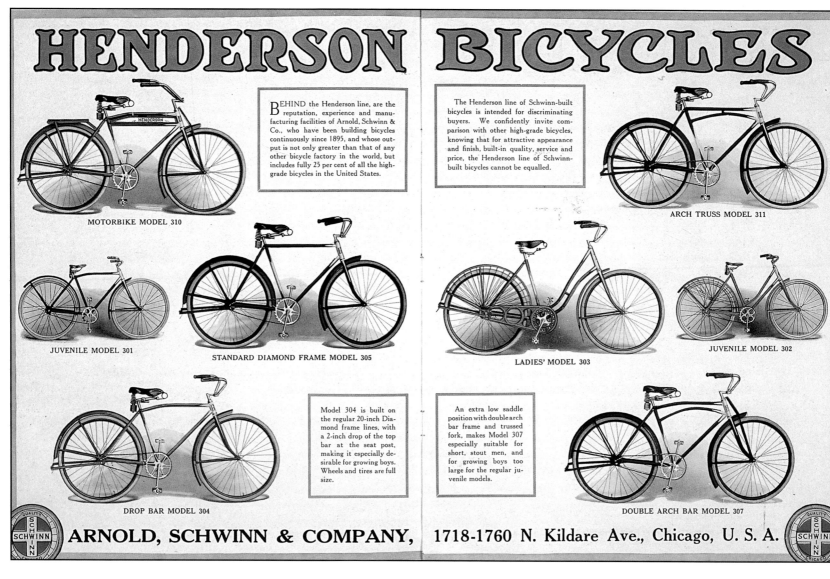

HENDERSON BICYCLES

BEHIND the Henderson line, are the reputation, experience and manufacturing facilities of Arnold, Schwinn & Co., who have been building bicycles continuously since 1895, and whose output is not only greater than that of any other bicycle factory in the world, but includes fully 25 per cent of all the high-grade bicycles in the United States.

The Henderson line of Schwinn-built bicycles is intended for discriminating buyers. We confidently invite comparison with other high-grade bicycles, knowing that for attractive appearance and finish, built-in quality, service and price, the Henderson line of Schwinn-built bicycles cannot be equalled.

MOTORBIKE MODEL 310

ARCH TRUSS MODEL 311

JUVENILE MODEL 301

STANDARD DIAMOND FRAME MODEL 305

LADIES' MODEL 303

JUVENILE MODEL 302

Model 304 is built on the regular 20-inch Diamond frame lines, with a 2-inch drop of the top bar at the seat post, making it especially desirable for growing boys. Wheels and tires are full size.

An extra low saddle position with double arch bar frame and trussed fork, makes Model 307 especially suitable for short, stout men, and for growing boys too large for the regular juvenile models.

DROP BAR MODEL 304

DOUBLE ARCH BAR MODEL 307

ARNOLD, SCHWINN & COMPANY, 1718-1760 N. Kildare Ave., Chicago, U. S. A.

Above and Opposite
While the Schwinn family flourished in the motorcycle business, the bicycle company was struggling with thin margins and low profits. Still, bicycle output remained substantial, and the line seemed endless as the Henderson and Excelsior names joined the World line to capture the not-yet-ready-for-motorcycles clientele.

The motorcycle division never materialized—like similar unrealized hopes for bicycles on the battlefield. Still, Ignaz Schwinn found a reliable market for his motorcycle, a healthy percentage of which went to police departments, particularly the Chicago force which had them painted blue. (Until 1920 most motorcycles were olive green, a holdover from the military days.) Big Hendersons in particular were effective at enforcing traffic laws in cities and towns where streets were increasingly clogged with "tin lizzies."

Still, there were signs that the motorcycle boom might hit a brick wall, as bicycles had done a quarter-century before. Henry Ford was doing what he intended to do, putting the automobile within reach of "the multitudes," and by 1929, a Henderson at $435 cost about the same as a Model A. While police business remained brisk even into the Depression, that business would shrink as well when automobile radios and police bands

were developed and made squad cars the enforcement vehicle of choice by the next decade.

Then there were the troublesome Henderson brothers. Will left the company and proceeded to violate a non-compete clause in the original Henderson sale, then grieved everyone who knew him when he was killed riding his fast, new Ace Four in Pennsylvania in 1922. Tom left a substantial debt with Schwinn when he quit, and though Ignaz forgave it, this was just another problem that made Ignaz think fondly of retirement.

"Gentlemen, Today We Stop"

Ignaz Schwinn, a bicycle man at heart, was increasingly aware that motorcycles were a different and sometimes dangerous beast. Thus, Schwinn must certainly have felt apprehension when he followed other motorcycle manufacturers with the sponsorship

continued on page 45

WORLD BICYCLES

ARCHED TRUSS MODEL 111

RACING MODEL—5-R MADE IN ALL OUR LINES

DOUBLE ARCH BAR MODEL 107

DROP BAR MODEL 104

THE World Bicycles constitute the oldest line made by Arnold, Schwinn & Co. This bicycle was nationally known more than a quarter of a century ago, as a staunch, high-grade machine. It was very speedy on the racing paths, and the exploits of the famous "World Racing Team" gave it a wide and lasting reputation.

Jobbers and dealers are especially invited to look over the World line at the Show.

For general attractiveness, finish, equipment, built-in quality and popularity, the World line is a sure winner. Behind the reputation of the World bicycle, is the long and honorable manufacturing record of Arnold, Schwinn & Co. Several years ago, Mr. Schwinn turned out his millionth bicycle in the present factory. From the development of the bicycle in 1882 up to the present day, Mr. Schwinn has built millions of bicycles and they have all been good bicycles.

DIAMOND FRAME MODEL 105

Juvenile Model 101 is built along regular bicycle lines in junior sizes with 14, 16 and 18-inch frames; of sturdy construction throughout.

DROP BAR MODEL 104

LADIES' MODEL 103

MOTORBIKE MODEL 110

Juvenile Model 102 is a regular ladies' model built especially for small girls; an appropriate companion for Model 101.

ARNOLD, SCHWINN & COMPANY, 1718-1760 N. Kildare Ave., Chicago, U. S. A.

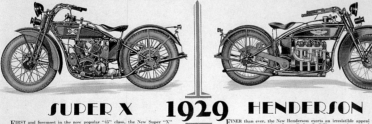

By the 1920s, the Excelsior name was used on the V-twins of the Schwinn-owned motorcycle lines while Henderson was the moniker carried by the four-cylinder model.

The 1925 Excelsior Super-X was an advanced street motorcycle, but it was particularly successful on the track and in hill climbs as well. It was probably on a machine like this that Excelsior-sponsored racer Bob Perry was killed—an event that dampened Ignaz Schwinn's enthusiasm for motorcycles, and perhaps for business in general.

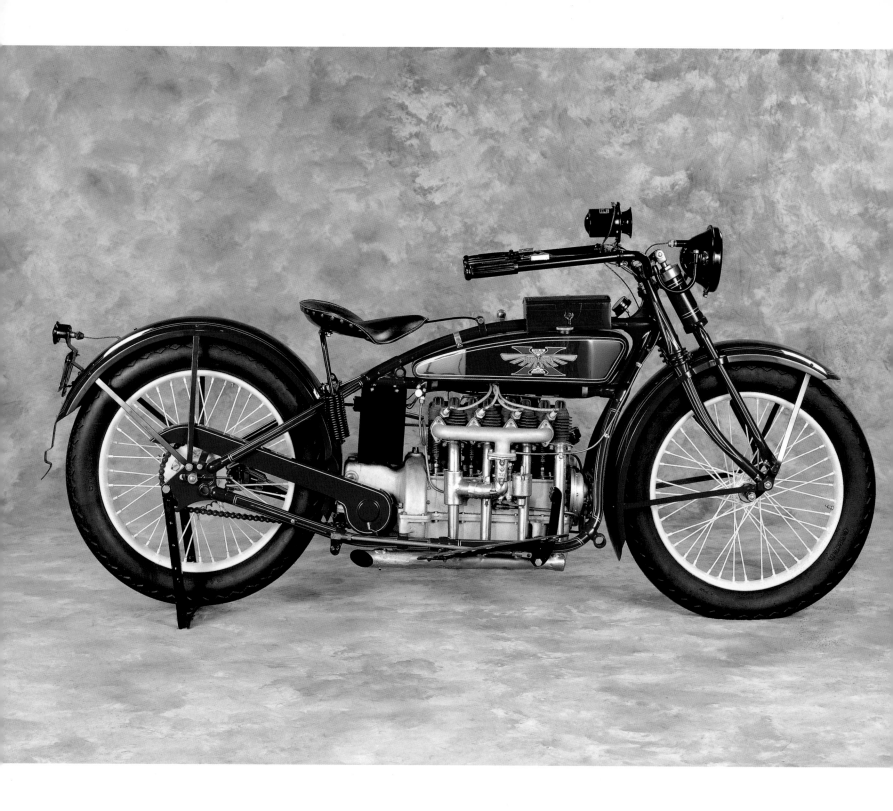

44

Continued from page 40

of a racing team with daredevil riders circling dirt- and board-track ovals in cities across the country. But for Excelsior, there was little choice in the matter, as racing was a major public attraction and indispensable for promoting a line of motorcycles.

"Here are a few of the racing men who have pinned their faith to Good Old X and have thereby gained in money and reputation," stated an Excelsior sales brochure in 1916. And despite the heavy frames that Will Henderson scorned, the Excelsior team set records at a steady clip. It clocked the first official speed of 100 miles per hour, a record of which Ignaz was naturally proud.

Then, in the middle 1920s, another motorcycle tragedy occurred that affected the Schwinns deeply. The tragedy involved one of the stars of the Excelsior team, Bob Perry, who, as one brochure stated, "won his title 'King of the Dirt Tracks' on an 'X,' and in spite of many brilliant inducements, has stuck to the machine that Always Makes Good." One reason Perry remained with the "X team" was because Ignaz had identified him as a talented engineer and was putting him through technical school. It all ended one day on a board track in California. Perry was warming up for a race later that day. On a banked turn he had what seemed like an innocent brush with another rider. But inexplicably, the two got seriously tangled. Perry crashed and was killed. When the news reached Chicago, Ignaz took it nearly as hard as if it were his own son. The Excelsior racing team was shut down shortly thereafter.

Beyond events such as the death of Henderson and Perry, there were other dark clouds over the motorcycle business at the time—the market and eventually the economy. Clearly, the public's fascination had turned to automobiles, and then came the Depression, a blow that the industry, which had grown so fast so recently, could ill-afford. The story of Excelsior's end began with a trip that Ignaz took to Washington to discuss the economic outlook in 1931. It was very bad, he was told by the economic experts, and Schwinn did not need to be told that it was particularly bad for a company that depended upon yearly improvements and a measure of planned obsolescence.

The Depression had already been difficult for Ignaz Schwinn. He was an active trader in the stock market, and the crash had taken a heavy, though not disabling, toll. In the midst of these troubles, he had discussed the sale of his motorcycle company with the chiefs of General Motors, but there was enough fear in Detroit to put the brakes on any such plan.

Thus, when Ignaz came home from Washington, he called his closest employees together and made his announcement in his frank, inimitable way. "Gentlemen, today we stop." Excelsior, Henderson, and Super X motorcycles passed into history. Ignaz's employees were instructed to explain that it was not so much economic woes that caused the closing of Excelsior. Rather it was that Ignaz Schwinn needed and deserved a rest from the business world which, despite a few rough spots, he had mastered in many ways. And it was a long retirement, happily, as the founder lived for another 17 years until 1948.

Opposite
1925 Henderson Deluxe. By 1925, Schwinn had made minor changes to the Henderson, including blue paint—different from the earlier standard of military green and preferred by at least one large segment of the Henderson market: police departments.

By 1931, Ignaz Schwinn was ready to retire. The Depression had taken the wind out of the motorcycle market's sails, so he closed Excelsior, leaving the bicycle company to his brilliant and ambitious son Frank.

Chapter Four

BALLOON-TIRE QUALITY

Not everyone employed by Ignaz Schwinn in 1931 was ready to retire, and even after the closing of Excelsior, there was still a business to manage. Among the survivors from Excelsior was Frank Schwinn, who had proved himself to be a motorcycle engineer par excellence, and was young enough—he was 36 at the time—to make his mark in his father's first love, which was bicycles.

Frank W. Schwinn, or "Frank W.," as he was often called, constituted the essential second act in a family business that became an empire. He inherited his father's passion for the business and continued his entrepreneurial spirit. At the same time Frank W. had the sophistication, some would say genius, to see where the bicycle business might go and how to get it there.

Frank W. proved from an early age that he was a natural in the cycle trade. After high school, he enrolled in the engineering program at Chicago's Armour Institute (later Illinois Institute of Technology) to prepare for Arnold, Schwinn and Excelsior. It turned out, however, that there was little the school could teach him about bicycles and motorcycles that he was not experiencing firsthand. He never graduated.

An instinctive sense for building things was the gift that Frank W. received from his father. Ignaz himself was known for sauntering into the old factory and making design changes in his bicycles by drawing them in the dirt floor with his cane. For the son, making pictures of new ideas came naturally as well, and over the years, the company's thousands of innovations in frames, wheels, and components, were conceived on sketch pads

BING CROSBY AND HIS BOYS . . . all riding Schwinns! Master Lindsay's riding the handlebars of Bing's Schwinn-Built Lightweight, with Gary next, and the twins, Dennis and Phillip bringing up the rear. The famous radio and screen star writes: "Schwinns gets our vote for its written Lifetime Guarantee. When a maker does that, it's got to be good."

that Frank W. kept close to his desk and even carried with him when he traveled.

If anything separated Frank Schwinn from his father it was that the son possessed a worldliness obvious to anyone who knew him. Young Schwinn was a great reader on subjects of all kinds. He devoured volumes of religious philosophy, though he was not particularly religious. While he never wandered the world aimlessly—as other sons of wealthy men sometimes did at that time—he made far-flung travels in his mind by reading books about history, anthropology, and horticulture. Later in life he even obtained a copy of the Kinsey Report, the first detailed study of American sexual mores.

More to the point of the family business, young Frank Schwinn possessed an impatient spirit, and he was particularly impatient with the status quo of the bicycle industry, which was bumping along at a dismal level in 1931. With little direct evidence except his own ambition to back him up, he believed that Arnold, Schwinn & Co., still a relatively obscure name in the trade, might do more than rise to the top of the bicycle market, which then was not growing at all. Frank W. Schwinn was determined to expand that whole idea of bicycles and maybe even make them boom again as they did in the 1890s.

There were many obstacles, however. Quality-wise, the American bicycle had fallen to an "irreducible minimum," as Frank W. often described it. And poor bicycle quality, he insisted, was only partly due to the buying public's lack of interest. The industry itself was more fully to blame.

Left
The Aerocycle's detailing would have satisfied just about any wannabe motorcyclist. Its horn, controlled by a handlebar switch, was the envy of just about the whole bicycle crowd. At $34.95, however, it was a heavy hit for dads and led to slightly more modest machines in 1935 and later.

Above
By 1941, movie stars of the first rank were signed up to push Schwinns, and in many cases their kids were, too. "Cyclorama" was the name of the brochure that youngsters could send for and show to their parents–they would then demand a Schwinn and no other.

Arnold, Schwinn & Co.

Introduces Super Balloon Tire Bicycles

**LOW PRESSURE
18 to 22 Lbs.**
According to weight of rider

The only major development since the coaster brake—on the finest specially constructed bicycles built by the oldest and most outstanding American manufacturer. A 2⅛″ automobile type double-tube, straight-side, cord tire—on a new deep drop center rim—a construction embodying all the latest advancements in the tire art.

ARNOLD, SCHWINN & CO.
1718 NORTH KILDARE AVE.
CHICAGO, ILLINOIS
TELEPHONE BELMONT 6793

MODEL B10E

The B10E, the original balloon-tire bicycle, was modeled in 1933 after the durable bicycles that Frank W. Schwinn saw in Germany. It was inspired by his impatience with the dismal quality of most American bicycles of the 1920s and early 1930s.

On the retail side, chain stores such as Western Auto and Sears dominated on the basis of cutthroat pricing and their ability to offer time payments. Independent dealers, who more fully appreciated bicycles, might have stood for quality, but they had almost no power in the marketplace.

Beyond pressures on the retail side, the impulse to improve quality was next to impossible due to the control that the parts suppliers exercised over the industry. The few American companies that supplied the manufacturers with tires, coaster brakes, chains, and other essentials enjoyed virtual monopolies in their lines, which meant that they had little incentive to improve their product and alter what was undoubtedly a profitable situation for them. And without help from the suppliers, it would be difficult for anyone to build a better product.

Frank W., meanwhile, insisted that he was the exception. Most manufacturers in this period had no desire to have their names on merchandise they knew was shoddy. But Schwinn did its best to maintain a standard that was frankly unappreciated. "The company had, for many years, used a small round transfer marked 'Schwinn Quality' which it would surreptitiously stick on the frame until ordered to leave it off, and usually it was ordered off," Frank W. wrote years later. It was a symptom of the bicycle's irreducible minimum—selling on the basis of good workmanship was generally unthinkable.

As a former motorcycle man, Schwinn was keenly aware of the cheap steel, shoddy brazing, and fall-apart parts that were almost everywhere in the bicycle industry. For a good two years, Frank Schwinn found himself almost powerless to do anything about it; chain store prices and low-quality parts were smothering almost any thought to do better. Schwinn's impatience came to a head, however, in 1933 when he returned from a business trip to Germany. There, he saw a healthy bicycle industry that had developed a strong and utilitarian bicycle for the rough cobbled streets of German cities. It used something called the "balloon tire," entirely more durable than the "glorified garden hose" that was used on American bikes and which Frank W. so despised. The balloon tire was double-tubed, like the auto tire. Not only did it hold up longer, but also it was easier to repair by simply patching or changing the inner tube.

Now inspired with the idea to build a new American balloon-tire bicycle, Schwinn made contact with his rim and tire suppliers who were enjoying virtual monopolies at this time. They hardly gave the young bicycle maker the time of day. "The U.S. Rubber Company definitely and emphatically dismissed the 'silly idea' on the ground that they had, some years ago, tried to build wire bead tires [like the balloon tires on automobiles] and failed," Schwinn wrote. Schwinn's counter argument that they were successfully made in Germany was dismissed with a huff that might have discouraged a less determined manufacturer.

Almost out of spite, Frank W. persisted. He was successful at getting Firestone, with whom Schwinn had good relations from the motorcycle days, to duplicate the

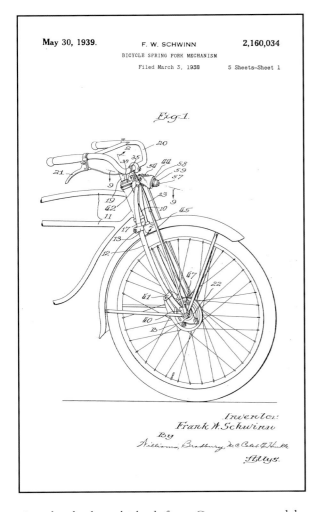

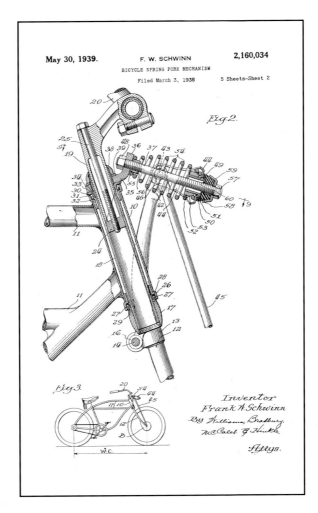

Among scores of patents awarded to Frank W. Schwinn in his long career was the spring fork for balloon-tire bicycles. It was "conceived, designed, engineered, manufactured, and guaranteed" (as noted in the 1938 catalogue) by Schwinn just before World War II placed a halt on production of anything but the most basic bicycle. In postwar America, the spring fork helped make the Black Phantom the bicycle of choice for a generation of kids.

rims that he brought back from Germany as models. Next he convinced Fisk Rubber to accept an order for tires—enough for 5,000 bicycles. Unfortunately, Fisk failed to copy the German tire properly, and with ultimate audacity, Schwinn went back to U.S. Rubber. "Make tires, or I'll import them," he said.

Something in Schwinn's tone turned the rubber maker's head, and it produced tires that were a close match of the German ones. In the meantime, Schwinn fashioned a frame for the new and revolutionary bicycle he had in mind. Frank W. later wrote: "The heretic [as he called himself] widened out his frames and fork, got out a balloon tire model—told the truth about it in the one and only trade paper, and hoped for the best. The result was both interesting and amusing."

As expected, the chain stores snickered at the idea. Too expensive, they said. Too heavy. They were happy with their bicycle trade, apparently, and preferred not to rock the boat. Little did they know that Frank W. Schwinn was about to rock it permanently. Schwinn found at least one important wholesaler in the field to cooperate with his idea. The Chicago Cycle Supply

Company "saw the light, got religion and sent his disciples—his sales force—out to preach the Gospel." Chicago Cycle sold enthusiastically, though with one restriction: Frank Schwinn prohibited them from selling to price-cutting chain stores. His rule for wholesalers was that independents and independents alone were to benefit from the soon-to-be craze for balloon-tire bicycles.

The strategy fell into place like clockwork. Suddenly, the long-suffering neighborhood bicycle dealers had something that department-store rivals could not get: Schwinn's original balloon-tire model, the B-10E. The independent "paid the few dollars per each more, and sold them pronto," Schwinn wrote. "In three months, the double-tube balloon tire and metal rim were a soaring success and in twelve months it was practically standard for the industry."

These events quickly changed the industry. By 1934, other manufacturers were building balloon-tire bicycles—big retailers got them and tried to dominate as before. Fortunately for Schwinn, the "heretic" who conceived the concept maintained the lead. Finally, independent bicycle dealers—who were still in back alleys

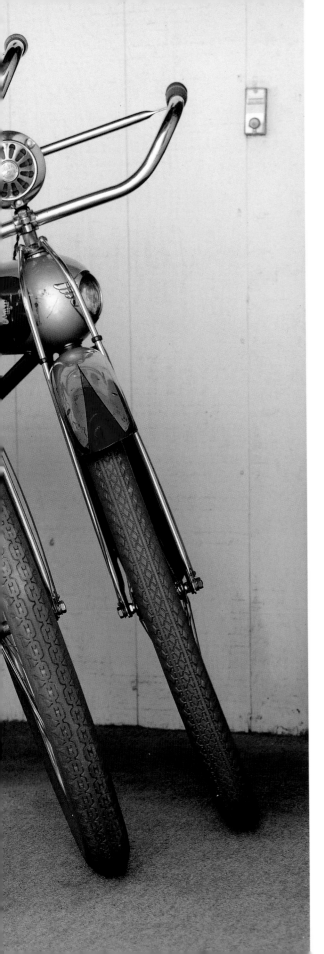

sharpening lawn mowers—had power. Quality and durability were talking points in bicycle sales, and small retailers who really knew bicycles could give this talk better than anyone else. The independents also had the advantage of selling something built by Schwinn, as the name was steadily built up in the public's mind.

In general, "Schwinn-Built" bicycles, as they became known, did not just bring a larger part of the market to the still-small Chicago manufacturer, it expanded the bicycle market significantly. Bicycles, once considered a product of short useful life, were now a more durable investment. Moreover, balloon-tire bikes now had more in common with motorcycles and automobiles. That meant "children went for the balloon tires in a big way," Schwinn wrote. "There was romance in it! The motor car industry had been publicizing balloon tires for years—they were on all the cars. The combination of improved quality and a wildly upgraded image put Schwinn at the head of an entirely new era in the bicycle business."

It was still a highly competitive, even chaotic, trade. Schwinn itself continued to produce bicycles for dozens of different retailers including B.F. Goodrich auto stores, which got direct shipments. (Frank W.'s rule

Streamlining at a slightly more attractive price was behind the introduction of the Motorbike, aka Cycleplane, in 1935.

The 1934 Streamline Aerocycle featured balloon-tire durability with the most up-to-date styling. Sales were not stunning—it was too expensive. Still, the appeal of the Aerocycle, even if unattainable by most, helped create a demand for Schwinns that continued for more than a generation.

against chains applied, clearly, to wholesalers but not to himself.) Many stores and nearly every wholesaler wanted its own nameplate—over 100 head tags were going on Schwinn bicycles at this point—which meant that the only way for Arnold, Schwinn to stay atop the balloon-tire phenomenon was to continue innovating. This meant better quality but also classier styling as well.

In fact, yearly model changes came naturally to the Schwinn engineering department, which was dominated by Frank W. For them, motorcycles were a thing of the past, but streamlined styling looked just as becoming on a big balloon-tire bicycle. Indeed, modern streamlining was in vogue in all aspects of design in the 1930s, from automobiles to toasters. The lesson was not lost on Frank Schwinn.

Thus, the Aerocycle of 1934 represented a major turning point in bicycle history, actually one of several that would come in that decade. For the first time since the Gay 90s, the look of the bicycle was suddenly and radically changed. Schwinn promoted the Aerocycle for "the grace and beauty of the newest air liner." It featured a teardrop-shaped "tank" covering the crossbar and truss, inside of which was a tool compartment and place for a cell battery to run the taillight and horn. It had the sleekness of a true and utterly up-to-date motorcycle.

The Aerocycle became a most desirable bicycle— and remains one among collectors—but not a best seller. It was too expensive for the market at the time. While everyone agreed that this was a breakthrough design and widely coveted by youngsters for its "streamlined beauty" (in the words of a Schwinn copywriter), Schwinn's next objective was to produce something not too different but which more people, more parents, could afford. That came the next year, 1935, in the Cycleplane. This balloon-tire model had more basic assembly and less intricate details, but it boasted many of the Aerocycle's coveted features, including elaborate electrical equipment and a tank that contained the battery.

Velocipedomania Redux

By the most obvious measures, Schwinn was marvelously successful in these years. Unit sales jumped from 86,000 in 1934, to 107,000 in 1935, then to 201,000 the following year. In fact, Schwinn's market share did not rise quite so wildly again after going from 6.6 percent to 14.7 percent in 1933. Other manufacturers such as Columbia and Huffman (later Huffy), imitating the balloon-tire craze, were enjoying increases of their own.

Still, Schwinn emerged as the indisputable leader in other ways. New styles and new features normally came first from Schwinn—credit for which went to old motorcycle designers, according to Frank

Alfred Berghouse's bicycle store in Kankekee, Illinois, was hardly typical of the independent dealer in the 1930s— most had a dusty and distinctly unsalesman-like look. But Berghouse was the kind of knowledgeable bike salesman that Frank W. Schwinn wanted to encourage when he decided to market his revolutionary balloon-tire models through the independents and cut off most chain-store discounters.

In 1937, Schwinn brought out the expander brake, adapted from the motorcycle, a feature that promoted Schwinn as not just the most desirable bicycle on the road but also the safest.

Opposite
Between 1933 and World War II, Schwinn introduced dozens of true technical innovations, many of them borrowed from the old days of Excelsior motorcycles. The expander brake promoted smooth and safe riding and was not at all commonplace in neighborhoods where bicycles, especially Schwinns, and their many features were significant status symbols.

to his competition. Better steel tubing was one expensive improvement over run-of-the-mill bicycles. (Frank Schwinn was not shy about saying that some competitive bicycles were downright dangerous.) Another improvement by 1934 was electric welding, forerunner of the patented "flash welding" which used electric current, not a torch, to create a stronger joint. Other makers also approximated this technique, which was borrowed from the aviation industry. (Huffman described their Streamliner of this period as "aircrafted.") But no one else promoted the safety and durability of their frames as successfully as Schwinn.

Another improvement of this period, also in the frame, became one of Schwinn's most enduring innovations of the 1930s. This was the "cantilever" design, a relatively simple change from the previous standard bicycle frame. The most obvious advantage of the cantilever frame was in its styling. It was gracefully streamlined with the rear fork sweeping forward and curving unbroken as the supporting truss beneath the top bar. The cantilever frame was not only sleeker than previous models, it was considerably sturdier as well. Here again, the idea for this important patented feature belonged directly to Frank W., who drew it on a pad and delivered it to a mechanic or engineer for prototyping.

W. who wrote that they "were schooled in a business where annual model changes and improvements were the rule." In fact, Frank W. still ruled the design end of the business, continuing to sketch improvements by himself, then handing them to draftsmen and patent attorneys. The "knee-action spring fork" represented just such an advance in Schwinn's 1938 line. An obvious adaptation of a motorcycle suspension, it was much appreciated by children not yet ready for a Harley-Davidson.

Schwinn led the way in devising and producing many other components and accessories of the period as well. Expander brakes (another old motorcycle feature) and caliper brakes were either designed or fabricated in-house. Drop forging was done in the plant for parts in which strength was key, such as handlebar stems and seat posts. Rims, taillights, headlights, chain guards, and the famous "Cycelock" (with a key in the steering head) were either made in-house or by exclusive arrangement.

Such "bells and whistles" on bikes made by Arnold, Schwinn & Co. were the natural eye catchers for both dealers and customers. Yet other elements of the product were also important in setting a "Schwinn-Built" bike apart from the competition. One was the quality of the frame, which always stood apart from "chain-store pottage," as Frank W. rancorously referred

The Lifetime Guarantee

While successful innovation by the company in this period remained the work of Frank W.'s extremely fertile imagination, there was nothing mysterious about the marketing success of Schwinn. The most important thing that Frank W. ever did in selling Schwinn-Built bicycles came in 1939 when he introduced a lifetime guarantee on the frame and many of the parts. This was something that none of the competition had yet dared to do, yet Frank W. did not regard the move as risky. While the standard in the industry was a one-year guarantee, Schwinn rightly believed that any welded or metal part, if it were going to fail at all, would very likely fail in the first year anyway. This logic was combined with a conviction that he held all his life: "I'd rather have 99 of 100 customers take advantage of me than have one customer not treated right," he said many times.

The lifetime guarantee not only increased sales by hundreds and thousands, it created a reputation for Schwinn-Built bicycles that changed the nature of the market. Suddenly, the manufacturer's name, previously hidden behind the retailer's nameplate, began to appear from store to store and town to town. The Schwinn name was a selling point, and among other things that this achieved for Arnold, Schwinn & Co., it encouraged them to spend more money on advertising.

By 1938, even B.F. Goodrich, another one of Schwinn's chain-store customers, was asking for Schwinn "Seal of Quality" stickers, and salesmen knew they helped sell bikes. The following year, they were hanging the lifetime guarantee on the handlebars, which naturally ended any argument about whether or not the Schwinn name built traffic in the store. Bicycles manufactured by Schwinn were now retailed as Schwinn-Built, often along with the retailer's head tag. The rise of Schwinn's name in the stores "proved of advantage to both parties concerned," wrote Frank Schwinn some years later. It created a whole new relationship between manufacturer and retailer: "close cooperation, consideration of each other's problems which were openly and honestly discussed."

Along with the Schwinn name, the company's approach to sales and distribution evolved in ways that other bicycle makers had never really considered. Most importantly, they continued to promote the interests of the independent bicycle dealer, which Frank Schwinn saw as the company's most indispensable lifeline to the customer. Strong dealerships, Schwinn learned early on, linked makers of bicycles more closely to the public that bought them.

This realization was anything but obvious as the Depression loosened its grip in the mid-1930s; marketing costs were a luxury that most companies did not indulge. But Frank Schwinn cultivated the dealer network, doing on a smaller scale what the large automakers were doing with great care and skill. As Ford and General Motors succeeded at making partners of its retailers, so did Schwinn, and the success of the Chicago bicycle maker became one of the great "family-business" stories of the era.

Left
The 1940 D-97X0 was just about as basic a balloon-tire bike as Schwinn sold. Still, there was always a broad selection of colors—black, blue, brown, green, maroon, or red—and some even had rims to match.

The Hollywood. The name would be used on a variety of girl's models for a generation to come, but the first Hollywood was described in the catalogue with features such as truss fork, chrome chain guard, and horn button with concealed wiring—everything the boys in the neighborhood were getting in the Schwinn Auto-Cycles of the time.

1952 B2E. When this child's 20-incher was built, the Schwinn mark was in demand and adorned the tank in prominent script.

1941 Auto-Cycle Deluxe. This "cantilever-frame beauty" was "unequipped." An equipped version had a fender-light and tank with electrical equipment inside. The many Schwinn models of the classic balloon-tire era were all developed in the interest of finding the right price for every rider.

Below

Girl's balloon-tire bicycles, like the boy's models, came with a selection of different features. Hollywoods in 1941 came with spring fork and expander brake if desired. Most had the fender-light, adding "a touch of streamlining which changes the appearance of the entire bicycle," the catalogue pointed out.

AI. LETOURNEUR

Chapter Five

UPHILL ON LIGHTWEIGHTS

Frank W. Schwinn, who delighted in referring to himself as "the heretic," had almost single-handedly revolutionized the bicycle industry with the balloon-tire concept. With that success behind him, the heretic believed he could take another step forward and perhaps bring back shades of the 1890s bicycle boom. That step was the "lightweight" bicycle, which Schwinn hoped would return the bicycle as an adult pastime and perhaps even an indispensable mode of transportation.

Lightweights were much on Schwinn's mind when he made another trip to Europe in 1935. While there, he was impressed by a segment of the industry that was prospering with bicycles that adults could ride enjoyably over long distances. Particularly in England, where asphalt roads had largely replaced cobblestones, throngs of adults had taken to riding on 1 1/4-inch wheels with three-speed internal-gear rear hubs.

Frank W. appreciated the careful engineering of these bicycles and notably those marketed by England's Raleigh Cycle Company. He also believed he could build something equal to the English models if not better, and that adults would take to them in America as they had in Europe. Schwinn returned home with several Raleighs and other makes plus a trunk load of spare parts. Back in Chicago he called his mechanical men together to discuss how a new Schwinn lightweight might be designed and built. The response in the factory was not encouraging, however. Manufacturing lightweights required different materials and new machines. Selling them meant finding buyers who didn't need a durable bicycle but a speedy one.

Yet Schwinn's desire to build bicycles for adults was no pipe dream. He insisted that a new lightweight market could be grown. Hollywood, for one, seemed enamored of the bicycle in the 1930s. For several years, the movie-star set, and particularly the "younger and pulchritudinous part," as Frank W. said, found bicycles a wonderful prop for publicity photos, which favored sleek bicycles for sleek young actresses. These were celluloid images, to be sure, but still hard to ignore.

Also at this time, rental bicycles proliferated in many cities around the country, and this got more adults on bicycles. There was a modicum of public support for this adult activity especially New York City, which one set aside times when bicycle riding was permitted and encouraged on the Coney Island boardwalk. Bicycle paths were hailed by some members of the press as progressive, though it plateaued rather quickly. Schwinn was determined to expand this activity with the right product. Most rental bikes, after all, "were heavy, cumbersome toys with which children could bump curb stones and not break up." To travel any distance, the majority of American bicycles of this period were hard-pedaling indeed. Not even the forced austerity of the Depression could overcome the fact that most bicycles on the American market were really designed for kids.

Left
Alf Letourneur, who enjoyed his fame on the track and with the night life crowd on two continents, made it onto a French postcard.

Above
Letourneur's feat continued to make a big impression in the 1950s when kids could pick up Schwinn comics at local dealers.

To most other American manufacturers, adults on bicycles was an idea whose time had not come. But Frank Schwinn was determined. He hatched a plan that was really an echo of the successful route his father had followed in the 1890s: a high-grade product that would quickly gain exposure and market share. Clearly, aggressive marketing of the World Cycle was critical to Arnold, Schwinn's early success, and at the crux of publicity at that time was racing, a formula Frank W. planned to duplicate.

Six-Day Racing

In the three decades since the World's glory days, bicycle racing had waxed and waned. But in the 1920s and 30s, the phenomenon of six-day racing had returned as one of the most popular spectacles in sports. At least twice a year, each of the biggest arenas in the biggest cities set up wooden tracks and brought in a dozen two-man teams to circle endlessly, break from treacherous jams, and engage in sprints along the way for cash and prizes called "premes." In the stands, some of New York's and Chicago's most fashionable night owls, as well as a good contingent of those cities' gangsters, were on hand to share in the excitement.

Frank Schwinn, as a cycling fan, enjoyed the pure grit of the six-day. As a businessman, too, he was impressed by the excitement that the events generated in the arenas and the daily press. He concluded that with company sponsorship and the mechanical skill he was sure he could apply to a good lightweight bicycle, Schwinn might make a name for itself on the track and parlay that name into healthy sales.

Six-day racing in this century was slightly less brutal than the "single sixes" of the late 1800s, when racers competed alone, riding for as long as 20 hours a day. The single sixes were wild and woolly events, with "whirling demons who ride between walls of shrieking faces," as the *New York Times* described a race in 1897. These races were eventually outlawed as inhumane, but "team sixes" grew popular in the Roaring 20s as promoters paid top riders hundreds of dollars a day and filled stadiums

every night and often in daytime hours as well. Some of the nation's great sporting palaces, such as Madison Square Garden (the second building of that name) and Chicago Stadium, were built in the 1920s with the certainty that six-day bicycle races reaped big revenues.

Riders of dogged determination, often on the edge of high-speed disaster, brought many fans to the arenas. But beyond the blood and guts, six-day promoters were skilled at keeping the long race interesting with premes, offered when an advertiser or big shot in the grandstands would offer 50 or even 200 dollars (". . . and a box of Arrow Shirts") for the winner of a mile or two-mile sprint. Premes always jolted slumberous riders into action. Devastating pileups, naturally, were common, as race officials urged riders to jam and elbow their way out of the pack, particularly when the grandstands were filled. It was often said that the American riders were tough, but that the Europeans were downright dirty. And promoters never discouraged such whispering, which naturally enraged Italian, Irish, and other immigrants—enough to get them to buy tickets and cheer for their countrymen.

The spectacle of the six-day also included the crowds in the grandstands where gangland figures in fine suits with flashy women were the most conspicuous. Al Capone was a big fan, for example, and his comings and goings were noted with as much interest as the whirling of riders on the track. (Capone offered rich premes, some said, but he always did so anonymously.) In New York, a fanciful episode in Jimmy Breslin's biography of Damon Runyon began when Runyon accompanied some unsavory New Yorkers to a race the night that gambler Arnold Rothstein was shot dead. It appeared, in this version of the tale, that Runyon's companions had some knowledge of the nature of Rothstein's demise, and with police looking to interview them, they reasoned they would blend in with the six-day crowd as nowhere else. It was a good plan except that several of the wise guys turned the spotlight on themselves by offering extravagant premes. As eyes turned their way,

they were forced to make a quick exit—the smartest thing that group did all night.

The Wastyns and the Paramount

Frank W. Schwinn believed that all this excitement could help sell lightweight bicycles, so he asked Emil Wastyn, a bicycle mechanic well known on the six-day circuit, to be a partner in the project. Wastyn had been building fine cycles for many of the top six-day riders for years, and he attended big Chicago races to perform the inevitable repairs that were needed in the heat of the race. Indeed, Emil and his son Oscar were ideal collaborators for Frank Schwinn. Not only were they experienced race-frame builders—Emil started in 1910 shortly after he

1940 New World. Named for the World cycle of turn-of-the-century fame, the New World was designed to develop a market for lightweights among touring adults at a lower price than the high-priced Paramount and slightly more moderate Superior. As always, Schwinn tried to fill every possible niche, with men's and women's models with coaster brakes, and others with caliper hand-lever brakes. (Front and rear caliper brakes, which Schwinn popularized in this country, were recommended for bikes with three-speed rear hubs, although no shifting mechanism is evident in this promotional painting.)

Enthusiasm for cycling was revived in the 1930s, partly by the austerity of the time and partly by the revolution in bicycles begat by Arnold, Schwinn & Co. Bike rentals became popular, as at this shop in Chicago, though it was a source of frustration to Frank W. Schwinn that most of the bikes people were riding were balloon-tire cruisers and not the lightweights that he believed would convert adults everywhere to the pleasures of pedaling.

immigrated from Belgium—they were also Schwinn dealers with an unshakable loyalty to the company and its owner.

The Wastyns started the Schwinn lightweight line with a design like the one they had been building for racers all along. Imported chromium molybdenum (chrome moly)—aircraft steel—would be used in the frame tubing. From that would be fashioned a lug frame of optimal strength and lightness. Geometry of relatively short wheelbase and a steep head angle was devised for the best acceleration and handling. Frank W. told the Wastyns to spare no expense in building

what would be introduced in 1938 as the Schwinn Paramount. Back at the factory, he put his metal shops to work making state-of-the-art components—crank sets of chrome moly, hubs machined to the closest tolerances, and sprockets drop-forged (not stamped) as was done by the best European bicycle manufacturers of the time. With Frank W. watching over the very shoulders of his machinists, these components, like Wastyn's frame, were an artistic success. Schwinn employees remembered the work as precise and time-consuming in the extreme—such that practicality

finally won out, and Schwinn went to Europe for many high-quality components.

It was soon apparent that the lightweight project had little chance of making any money. Nevertheless, Frank Schwinn not only turned out a line of Paramounts for racing and for the road, he also organized a team of some of the top six-day racers, mostly Americans, on the circuit. Though sponsorship meant little more at this time than a free bicycle and a jersey, Schwinn's racing program got off to a good start. Jerry Rodman, a six-day great of the late 1930s and early

1940s, was one of Chicago's best-paid pro athletes in his prime, but not so well paid that he turned down the offer of a good bicycle and the attentive service of Emil Wastyn. Nearly a dozen other top American riders followed suit.

Schwinn also contracted with the six-day promoters to put exhibits of Paramounts under the grandstands during the events. These spare racing machines were not displayed alone; Schwinn also showed off an ambitious line of road-touring lightweights. The Paramount Sports-Tourist was much the same machine as the racers used,

In the late 1930s, Frank W. Schwinn brought back shades of Schwinn's early racing glory with a team of six-day racers who made rooting for Americans on American bikes a patriotic pastime.

1937 Paramount (prototype). In 1937, Frank W. was anxious to build and sell lightweight bicycles. He joined forces with one of the nation's best-known bicycle mechanics, Emil Wastyn, in a bid to make the finest in the world. The result was the Paramount—built with chrome-moly tubing and equipped with the best components possible. Paramounts became the greatest American name in racing, though for decades it was an unprofitable labor of love.

In May 1941, Frank Schwinn and Emil Wastyn put daredevil racer Alfred Letourneur in high gear. Letourneur rode behind a midget race car on the flat, straight highway near Bakersfield, California, and set the amazing record of 108.92 miles per hour. Pilot of the midget race car was Ronney Householder, a former bicycle racer.

only with a longer wheelbase, upright handlebars, and a three-speed hub. Also on display was the Superior line, with domestic chrome-moly tubing and aluminum alloy in some components.

Schwinn's catalogues for these bicycles were elaborate with detailed specifications, exploded views of componentry, and letters from sponsored six-day riders. "We have ridden your new lightweights and have gone through the various parts with a fine tooth comb and are satisfied that you have the best bicycle that can be bought anywhere," wrote the famous team of Al Crossley and Jimmy Walthour.

Words paled in comparison to deeds, of course, and in December, 1938, the exciting news was reported that Bobby Thomas of Kenosha, Wisconsin, had won his first six-day race in Buffalo, New York, with German partner Gustav Kilian. Thomas was on a Paramount, and it was prominently noted that this was the first time since 1908 that a wholly American bicycle—frame and components—figured in a major six-day triumph.

Early the next year, Crossley and Walthour were on Paramounts for one of the most exciting races of the season. With an hour left to ride in Cleveland, the American Team, as they were called, was behind by a lap, a

By 1939, the best American six-day racers swore by Paramounts, and not only because Schwinn was a generous sponsor. Paramounts had everything top riders wanted in a track bike, including the services of leading race mechanics Emil Wastyn and his son Oscar.

Schwinn sponsored six-day racers and sometimes the races, as here in 1949 at the Chicago Amphitheater. Schwinn team member Cecil Yates is avoiding a big spill as the daredevil riders break out of a "jam"—something that happened countless times every night during a race.

mere 1/10 mile. Wearing bright Schwinn jerseys, they picked up their pace and, with the crowd roaring, made up the deficit and more. When the final bell rang, it was the first time that an American pair on American bicycles had won such a big race. The Schwinn Paramount received due, if not overblown, credit in the press.

100 Miles Per Hour on a Schwinn!

Frank W. next took an opportunity for the Paramount to go beyond the conventional racing circuit and get what he hoped would be some very big publicity. Whether it was Schwinn's idea or the Wastyns, the plan was to go for the most remarkable motorpace speed record ever. They would assault the almost preposterous speed barrier of 100 miles per hour on a bicycle.

As rider, they chose Alfred Letourneur, one of the most daring of the era's six-day riders, not to say one of the most unpredictable habitués of the clubs of Broadway and Rush streets. On the morning of May 17, 1941, Letourneur and his handlers drove out to a remote stretch of pavement near Bakersfield, California. Also present was Ronnie Householder, a former six-day rider and now a driver of midget race cars. Householder's racer was equipped with a windbreak behind which Letourneur would ride, gaining speed over the eight-mile strip, gradually getting up to 100 miles per hour or more. The bicycle involved in this bit of lunacy was no stock model, of course. It was a Paramount but with the front fork turned backward, which allowed the wheel to draw closer to the windbreak. The racer also had an enormous 57-tooth front sprocket and six teeth on the rear hub, creating a gear ratio of 9 1/2 to 1 (2 1/2 to 1 was normal).

Before attempting to break the 100-mile-per-hour mark, Letourneur and Householder took several warm-up runs and agreed on a strategy: Letourneur said that he could get to top speed by the fourth mile, and that is where the official timer should start clocking. By afternoon, Letourneur's first serious try at the 100-mile-per-hour mark came up short by just a few notches. Then late in the day, with an official from the American Automobile Association as witness, the driver and the rider hit the mile-long time trap at well over 100 and covered the distance at an official speed of 108.92 miles per hour.

Once again, Schwinn was at the center of a sensation with the desired result that buyers, when they perused bikes, would gravitate to the brand that set such a remarkable record. Indeed, Letourneur's record proved once again that Schwinns were durable, and his Paramount quickly went on tour to emphasize the point. Its

After the record-setting ride, Letourneur (in jersey) returned to celebrate with supporters at the shop of Hans Ohrt, one of the country's early dealers in lightweight and racing bicycles for the riding public.

Roller racing was a big sport in large and small auditoriums in the 1930s and 1940s. Here, Schwinn team members Cecil Yates (left) and Jerry Rodman (center) were hooked up to the dial that could make the crowds wild with excitement.

In 1948, roller-racer Lorette Burke was a state champion who sometimes rode exhibitions and showed that she could disrobe while keeping her Schwinn upright.

Opposite
Dorothy Lamour, one of the "pulchritudinous" Hollywood types who looked good beside a sleek bicycle, was one of the many stars signed up to endorse Schwinn lightweights in the 1940s.

Oscar Wastyn truing a wheel in the 1960s. After the decline of six-day racing, the Wastyn shop enjoyed the great bicycle boom of the late 1960s and 1970s which the Wastyns and Frank W. Schwinn had helped lay the groundwork for years before with America's best lightweight bicycles.

Near Right

The Wastyns, who built the first Paramounts in 1937, were true racing mechanics, but they had other clients as well, such as late-Vaudeville performer Paul Gordon whose sophisticated stage antics included bicycle acrobatics.

Far Right

By the 1960s, the Wastyns had seen it all, from the racing stars of old to the Apple Krate and Lemon Peeler. Here, Oscar Wastyn, Jr., and Sr. (left and center) are pictured with a friend outside their shop on Chicago's Northwest Side, not far from the Schwinn factory.

tires were torn nearly to shreds by the heat of high speed, but the frame remained gleaming, impressive, and a remarkably spare device to reach such an amazing speed.

Despite the publicity that Schwinn lightweights were getting, they returned discouraging sales, and Frank W. could only count them as a financial debacle, though a splendid one. For the next two decades, the domestic lightweight market never did catch on as Schwinn hoped. This gave him an opportunity do what he apparently enjoyed: admit gruffly that maybe he suffered from too-high ambition, but it was really the industry at large that was in the dark ages. "Paramount and Superior sales were a complete failure in spite of the costly 6-day racing team promotion, excellent trade promotion, etc.," Schwinn wrote. "The few Americans interested just did not believe that really good adult type cycles, or for that matter, any kind of top quality cycle could be produced in America."

Why? The sad truth was that bicycles, instead of getting more popular, were being forced off the roads in this period by the proliferation of automobiles, a trouble that began before World War II and continued afterward. The few bike paths in cities such as New York "died aborning because of patches of cycle paths here and there are meaningless . . . the cyclist must still run the enormous hazard of motorcar, truck, and streetcar traffic to reach them."

Frank W. Schwinn admitted disappointment but remained talkative on the subject of lightweight bicycles. He apparently enjoyed his attacks on other makers and the bicycle retailers who lacked interest in cultivating the adult market. "They just didn't know how and hadn't the faith and courage to spend the money to have a good job done for them," Frank W. wrote.

American lightweight bicycles would take another generation to catch on. When they did, Frank W. Schwinn was dead, but the legacy of the Paramount placed his company in a position to enjoy the great bicycle boom that hit in the late 1960s. By then the market was doing just about what Schwinn hoped it would when he and the Wastyns turned out a lightweight of the highest possible quality. He was imagining millions of adults riding bicycles for pleasure and transportation.

By the mid-1940s, movie stars were endorsing Schwinn lightweights. Ronald Reagan's agreement with Schwinn called for no remuneration—only publicity for the star and the studio—but Reagan insisted that he keep the bike.

Chapter Six

THE WAR YEARS

The long-term success of Arnold, Schwinn & Co., in retrospect, depended less on good times in the bicycle business than it did on what the company did when times were hard. An early example was Ignaz Schwinn's ambitious marketing and aggressive racing program in the waning days of the bicycle boom. Later, Frank Schwinn's development of the balloon-tire bike—a step taken against all odds—demonstrated definite resourcefulness in periods when bicycles were not all the rage.

Something similar can be said of Schwinn's continued commitment to lightweight bicycles. From the time Schwinn introduced them in 1938, lightweights were infuriatingly slow to catch on. Frank W. developed the Paramount and Superior lines with high hopes that the company might manufacture 5,000 of them each year. But in Frank W.'s lifetime they never came close to that.

Still, there was hope. The Depression certainly sparked new interest, as young people who might have been driving autos in more prosperous days were now getting around on bicycles instead. Much of this activity was out of necessity, but there was a growing cohort of happy enthusiasts as well.

Bicycle touring made gains in small but dedicated numbers all over the country, and for many reasons Schwinn's own backyard in Chicago seemed to be taking a lead. Touring got a big push in 1936 when Schwinn wholesaler Jack Hansen of Chicago Cycle Supply announced the first of many "bike trains" that were organized in the prewar period was scheduled for a morning run to Kankakee, an hour south, and would return that evening after a day of cycling in the country. A surprising 425 cyclists showed up for the event. Many

climbed right on to the baggage cars where someone had an accordion, and started dancing a Virginia reel.

Many of the group couldn't wait to do it again, and they did the very next Sunday, this time to Walworth, Wisconsin, near Lake Geneva. It was on the way back that evening that the old League of American Wheelmen showed signs of being reorganized. A Schwinn dealer from Evanston, Illinois, named Clarence Wanderscheid stood up in the rail car and told everyone that for the rest of the summer and fall, evening rides would start from his shop every Tuesday night. These became a popular weekly event, especially after people started fastening Lucifer lights, a Swiss-made generator lamp, onto their handlebars. And it was not long before the Evanston Cycle Touring Club was formed. It was one of the first chapters of the new L.A.W., which now had a strong contingent of cycling women as well.

A number of other touring clubs were affiliated with the L.A.W. by 1940, including the popular Columbus Park Wheelmen on Chicago's West Side. The Midwest's flatness may have had something to do with cycling's new popularity in the Windy City. Atmospheric pressure might have helped too, as "with-the-wind" rides were major summertime events for several of the local clubs. For these, members would meet in the morning; leaders tested the wind and chose their direction. They might start out for Warsaw, Indiana, about 100 miles southeast of Chicago. Then if a warm southerly breeze stirred up en route, they could easily change their destination and head north for Niles, Michigan, where frequent trains also were available to get them back to Chicago.

Left
Wartime production at the Schwinn factory included frames for airborne radar units. Military work kept the factory busy and ensured its readiness to return to bicycle building to meet the enormous pent-up demand caused by a four-year hiatus.

Above
Well before World War II, women were well-established in the Schwinn factory, as Ignaz Schwinn himself (no feminist) believed they were good and careful workers. During the war, government and military work required high security, and ID badges for all were de rigueur.

Ignaz Schwinn had long favored women in the brazing rooms of his bicycle factory. He believed they had the light touch necessary for the delicate process of assembling a frame. Schwinn's preference enabled his company to make a relatively easy transition from bicycles to wartime military work where women were needed to operate the production lines.

Other chapters of the L.A.W. sprang up throughout the country, and California was a natural hot spot for cycling. Weather was gentle, and if the terrain was more difficult than the prairies, there was a string of youth hostels along the West Coast that helped spawn some of the most tireless cyclists in the country. Word was that three members of a club from Southern California pedaled from the Mexican border to Canada and back in 47 days. And it did not escape notice that cycling in California, as everywhere else, became a custom of courtship for many young people at the time.

This kind of activity inspired Schwinn to persevere in lightweight bicycles, and in 1940, the company added the economical New World to its catalogue. The New World, named after the old World which was Ignaz Schwinn's first bicycle, was $32—less than the $75 Paramount and $50 Superior, and which the company happily compared to the price of an 1896 World Racer which was $125.

The New World featured some of the special components of the Superior, such as hubs of machined steel and light 1 1/4-inch rims. Options included a three-piece crank set, lighter, stronger, and tighter than the standard one-piece. Within a year of introduction, the New World also offered the Sturmey-Archer internal-gear three-speed hub. This constituted a monumental turning point in American bicycles, though hardly noticed at the time. The three-speed bicycle, long used in Europe, remained little-known in this country where bicycles, partly because of Frank Schwinn and partly in spite of him, were widely held as toys.

Cursing Demons

The bicycle market continued to present challenges to Frank Schwinn and company in the prewar years. One was the recession of 1938, the first serious economic downturn since the Depression, which took a heavy toll on the company. While 200,000 units sold in 1936, only 121,000 moved out the door in 1938. Frank Schwinn's first response, typically, was to curse the demons that worked against the bicycle business. He continued to complain, justifiably, that the latest increase in motorcar sales was literally squeezing bicycles off the roads. As a partial solution, Schwinn and his

company did what they could to support bicycle paths, even sending the great old-time racer Charlie "Mile-a-Minute" Murphy to help open one in New York. But a short stretch of cycle trail on the edge of a few cities, Frank W. knew, was little more than a lot of inconsequential "hullaballoo."

Still, Schwinn continued to invest despite hard times. In 1938, he put more than $1 million in the business. This was money, according to the Schwinn family, which he borrowed from father Ignaz, who was retired but still happy to appear at the office and in the factory (where he was known among the women working on production lines for his gentle but sometimes wayward cane).

Much of the new capital went into six "Conomatics," gear-driven machine tools that took plain steel bars and automatically carved precision parts for hubs, cranks, and other components. Conomatics represented some of the highest machine-tool technology of the day, and as Frank Schwinn took visitors around his plant, he liked to show off these ultramodern screw machines and point to the serial numbers. He had seven through twelve in his old factory on Chicago's

West Side. One through six, he was quick to note, belonged to General Motors.

Another important step forward was taken after one of Frank Schwinn's many trips to Europe. Schwinn maintained cordial relations with the heads of English, French, and German bicycle manufacturers, and with these men he complained of intermittent problems in

Right and Opposite
War work turned out to be family work at Schwinn as mothers, sisters, and cousins from nearby Chicago neighborhoods came in for jobs, many of which lasted for decades.

80

procuring sufficient steel tubing for production needs. When Schwinn discussed the issue with Sir George Wilson, chief executive of Raleigh Cycle Company and one of the old-line aristocrats of the bicycle business, Wilson suggested that the answer was to own the source of supply. Thus, when Schwinn arrived home he located and purchased a used tube milling machine. It was something unheard of in the American cycle industry at the time.

Other elements of Schwinn-Built bikes had similar stories in the late 1930s. Caliper brakes, Cycelock, handlebar stems, and the fender light were developed specifically for various models, many of them made in-house, others under contract with a trusted supplier, and always under Frank W.'s closest scrutiny. By 1940, no other American manufacturer actually produced as much of the bicycle in its own factory as Arnold, Schwinn & Co. did.

War and Schwinn Family Values

Not too long after Arnold, Schwinn achieved such standards of excellence, the company was forced to cease bicycle production. The United States entered World War II in 1941, and all healthy American factories were bidding for military-production business. Initially, many Chicago industries were disappointed that weapons contracts were slow in coming to the Midwest, but in Schwinn's case the government signed up the bicycle factory early. Several months before Pearl Harbor, welding and metal-working machinery in the company's plant at Kildare Avenue was hard at work turning out shells and many other parts for the war effort.

By 1942, all commercial bicycle production was discontinued, though the company had a contract for 10,000 bicycles a year for government use. These included a military bike, conspicuously drab, for riding on and around stateside bases. This contract also included a version of the Schwinn-Built Cycle-Truck, which featured a smaller front wheel to make room for a large basket, and was cleverly designed to place the load on the frame and not on the front fork. The wartime Cycle-Truck saw action mostly in mail delivery on Navy installations.

The folding bicycle was envisioned for paratroopers dropped behind enemy lines, though it was later determined that it might be more of a burden than a gain in a live battle situation.

20-mm and 40-mm shells on the Conomatics which previously cut and threaded ball-bearing cones and hub sets. The factory also made frames for airborne radar, tripods for machine guns, metal parts for aircraft cockpits, and "conduit elbows," which was watertight piping for electrical wire in ships.

Since Schwinn had all the contracts it could use during the war, its primary concern was labor. At least two years before the United States entered the war, enlistments and the draft were pulling many workers away. While several key employees received military deferments to operate essential machines, it was still up to general manager Bill Stoeffhaas to make sure that production would not run short. To do so, Stoeffhaas combined business with pleasure, spending more time watching one of his favorite sports, girl's softball.

That was how Dolly Becker began her 44 years with Schwinn. In 1939, Stoeffhaas had been following her team, which was sponsored by State Auditor Edward J. Barrett, and after a game he asked to see several of the players. Arnold, Schwinn was determined to field a top team for the industrial league, he told them, and playing ball for Schwinn also meant jobs in the plant. In fact, women had always worked at Schwinn, as Ignaz believed they had a better touch in the delicate process of brazing frames.

As men and women worked together on the production lines, the war had the effect of strengthening family values that were always important at Schwinn. Relatives of employees were welcomed and encouraged to apply for jobs at the factory, which was in the midst of Polish, German, and other ethnic neighborhoods on Chicago's Northwest Side. Especially during World War II, brothers, sisters, cousins, and even parents worked side by side. This, combined with the patriotic fervor that prevailed everywhere, kept Schwinn working smoothly for the duration of the war and for the generation that followed.

Another advantage of working at Schwinn was that employees felt a sense of "ownership" in their jobs—it was true long before anything like it became fashionable in labor relations. Phil Cicchino, who operated the Conomatics during and after the war, remembered that military work in the Schwinn plant was considered highly secret, and unauthorized personnel were prohibited. On occasion, Cicchino saw strangers looking through a box of finished shells; sometimes they were inspectors but he always challenged them directly. Another time, Cicchino told a man who was accompanying Frank W. in the factory to put out his cigar in the no-smoking area. Frank W. smiled sheepishly, something he seldom did, and later congratulated his machinist.

Also during this time, Schwinn attempted to get orders for a folding bicycle, an idea that went back to the old bicycle boom of the 1890s. In this case, the folding bicycle was designed for the backs of paratroopers who would benefit, it was thought, by having ready transportation upon hitting the ground. Fortunately for these brave soldiers, they were never saddled with this added bit of equipment, which weighed at least 30 pounds and probably more.

The majority of Schwinn's production capacity for the duration went into conventional weaponry. By the end of the war, it had produced tens of thousands of

If the Schwinn operation was a "family," however, there was never a question about who was running it. Once after the war, Cicchino was turning out bicycle parts, and Frank W. picked up one with a faint scratch. The boss complained, as he often did, and Cicchino was quick to reply that the cutting metal in the machine tool was not the best that could be used for the purpose. Schwinn disagreed. "You have to change that blade more often," said Frank W. who won the debate, of course, though Cicchino noted that after Mr. Schwinn died, and sons Frank V. and Richard took over, he finally convinced management to change the metal in the blade. It turned out to be both cheaper and more durable.

The Wonderful Whizzer

War work was all consuming for Schwinn, but Frank W. kept his eye on the bicycle market that would resume in earnest in 1946. He wanted to get his old standbys back in production, and he had some new designs in mind as well. Schwinn also took an interest in a product that achieved considerable popularity during the war, the Whizzer, a motorized bicycle that had a short, happy life in the 1940s and 1950s.

Whizzers were the creation of a small engineering company in Los Angeles that was lucky enough to get approval by the War Production Board. Primarily, they

During the war, the Army-Navy E-Award was given to military contractors who met production goals and otherwise served the government at a high level. Arnold, Schwinn & Co., received its "E" Flag in a ceremony on June 9, 1944. Even though there were 233 such awardees in Chicago during the war, the flag was flown with extreme pride, and Frank W. Schwinn (shown here behind the microphone) made sure no one forgot that his company was among them.

Frank W. Schwinn designed this Quadracycle with disabled veterans in mind—it was sturdy and remained stable even on an uneven track. While at least one hospital ordered a few Quadracycles, it was not sufficient to tool up the factory in the early postwar years when demand for conventional bikes was keeping the Schwinn factory very busy indeed.

manufactured four-stroke engines that could be attached to standard heavy-duty bicycles, and the board agreed that such a motor, costing $129.95 and getting 125 miles per gallon, could help solve gasoline- and rubber-supply problems on the home front.

Unfortunately, bad management burdened the Whizzer Motor Company from the beginning, and after the war it was purchased by a pair of entrepreneurs who moved the operation to Pontiac, Michigan. Whizzer soon became a good customer of Schwinn, as the cantilever

frame seemed custom-made for the company's complete kit—the motor fit neatly in the triangle under the seat while other bicycles required considerable bending to get it right. Moreover, propulsion at a top speed of 40 miles per hour required frame strength that Schwinns had and others did not.

Whizzer sales buzzed along, and by 1948 the company was selling over 200,000 units with Schwinn frames being used on many, though not all. Around this time Whizzer came to the logical conclusion that

it could save money by making its own frames, and Whizzer did what no bicycle manufacturer ever had the nerve to do: it copied Schwinn's patented cantilever frame.

Almost instantly, Whizzer vice president Ray Burch got a call from Schwinn's Bill Stoeffhaas. "That's a patented frame," Stoeffhaas said, "and we're going to sue." This was a matter of some concern for Burch, as his company was small and could hardly stand up to the much larger Arnold, Schwinn & Co. But then, while Whizzer's people waited nervously for legal papers, Burch met Frank Schwinn at a sales conference.

Frank Schwinn did not dwell on the legal problems between them. Instead, he was intrigued by several things that Burch was doing to promote Whizzer sales. One was the fact that the small company was advertising in *Life* magazine, a large expense that the larger Schwinn company was reluctant to undertake at that time. Another was that Burch had traveled the

country continuously and was using a number of Schwinn's own retailers as agents.

Frank W. began bluntly, as always. "We think you should let Schwinn handle Whizzer sales," he told Burch.

Burch said no, thank you. The last thing he needed to do was hand over his hard-won network to someone else.

"Then we'll make our own motorbikes," Frank W. said. "We'll have someone make motors, and put our kits in every store in America."

"Well, it's a free country," Burch replied to the older man.

There was something about this exchange that Frank W. liked. "Let's go have lunch," he said.

Over lunch, conversation grew friendlier, and what was clear to both was that motorbike sales were not apt to grow indefinitely. Used cars—their supply increasing—were nearly as cheap as Whizzers. Beyond that, light motorbikes were getting a rash of bad publicity, as more cars meant more traffic accidents, and when a Whizzer was involved it was often tragic.

Yet Frank Schwinn seemed to have something else on his mind when they ended their first pleasant lunch together. It turned out to be getting Ray Burch to work for Schwinn. He knew that he needed someone who understood modern marketing—someone who could help make Schwinn prosper in the postwar economic boom that was certainly on the horizon. He believed that Ray Burch was his man.

Chapter Seven

THE BLACK PHANTOM ERA

Arnold, Schwinn & Co. grew marvelously in the post-war years, selling more than 400,000 bicycles in 1947 and going up nearly every year thereafter. But more striking than the numbers was the growth of Schwinn's image. For a generation of Americans, the name of Schwinn became synonymous with the American bicycle itself.

Few names in America have ever achieved such status. For two decades after the war, Schwinn dictated bicycle style in an era and to an age group that became very style-conscious indeed. Through expert marketing and an uncanny knack for knowing what kids would want to ride, Schwinn defined the bicycle business at a moment when baby boomers became consumers and the economy was poised for its most remarkable growth ever.

Schwinn's elevation to the status of American icon was achieved initially through the devices of Frank W., whose wide-ranging abilities enabled him to manage manufacturing in remarkable harmony with the sales side of the business. While he was an engineer by training, he also understood better than most how to sell bicycles, and the important edge that his company would acquire by forming close relationships with dealers.

Schwinn made one of his most critical marketing decisions as early as 1933 as he produced his first balloon-tire models. That was to concentrate on the independent bicycle dealers, long beleaguered and almost extinct before the B-10E and the later Auto Cycle revived them. Schwinn believed that his bicycles—of higher quality and slightly higher price than the chain-store "pottage" that he scorned—could overcome discounters only if knowledgeable dealers sold them. Thus began a long and mutually beneficial association between Schwinn and neighborhood bicycle shops. This relationship began, as Frank W. explained, when he refused to sell to most department stores. They had long rejected the concept of a higher quality and higher prices—much to their regret when the balloon-tire craze took off.

Schwinn's connection with the bicycle shops grew closer almost by accident, in the late 1930s, when one of his wholesaler-distributors in California teetered near bankruptcy. Instinctively, Frank Schwinn stepped in and took virtual control of all of the wholesaler's business. It was an emergency situation, but Arnold, Schwinn quickly established proper relations with almost all of the 160 bicycle dealers on the distressed wholesaler's list—shipping bicycles directly, billing, and "taking its chances on collecting," as Frank W. later wrote. Surprising to almost everyone in the bicycle trade, and to the dismay of other wholesalers who saw their part of the business at risk, this arrangement worked.

Schwinn called it "dealer-direct" business, and he sang its praises to anyone who would listen. It enabled the company to cut prices enough to help meet the competition of chain stores. It provided wider profit margins for the manufacturer and retailer both. Perhaps most importantly, it gave Arnold, Schwinn & Co. the opportunity to know its retailers on a one-to-one basis, which made all the difference in the company's understanding of how and

Left
1954 Phantom (green) 1959 Phantom (red). The Black Phantom had already made its mark in neighborhoods across America when Phantoms green and red were designed for riders who marched to a slightly different beat.

Above
It was no exaggeration that Phantoms were preferred nine to one over any other bike, though lucky youngsters who got them were faced with the sometimes difficult choice of color.

COLORS: RADIANT RED, BLUE & GREEN, BLACK ENAMEL. BOYS' 26" MODEL WITH 3-SPEED, 2-SPEED OR COASTER BRAKE.

In 1945, comic-book readers everywhere introduced to Speedy Wheeler who made the point that a bicycle was a necessity. This episode, shown here in rough artwork, appeared in *Wonder Woman, Mutt & Jeff, Green Lantern,* and a number of other comics in 1945.

why bicycles were really sold. "Two years of experience with the California group turned out so well as to make previous conceptions of this type of operation look ridiculous," Frank W. wrote.

Schwinn's dealer-direct organization might have evolved quickly. By 1941, Frank W. was planning a new

price structure and distribution system—keeping wholesalers in the picture only to take orders and stock spare parts, and perhaps even to provide financing for shops so customers could buy bikes and pay for them in installments. These plans were interrupted by the war, but the seeds of a new way of running the bicycle business were planted. Little by little, the people at the company in Chicago drew closer to dealers and customers. In fact, the wholesalers remained in the mix until the 1960s, when an antitrust decision against Schwinn forced distribution in-house. But very early in the postwar economic boom, Schwinn had its finger on the pulse of the market as very few companies had it in any industry in America.

An American Icon

Understanding customers, along with the ability to sell high-quality bicycles to kids, paid off handsomely in 1949. That year Schwinn came out with one of the great consumer products of the postwar era: the Black Phantom, coveted by hordes of youngsters throughout the 1950s (and by growing numbers of collectors today).

The Black Phantom made no claim to revolutionary engineering. It was not too different, in fact, from the prewar Auto Cycle and the B-6, which came out in 1946. But the Black Phantom quickly enjoyed a reputation for stylishness and desirability that no other bicycle ever really surpassed. While its streamlined parts were familiar, the lavish use of chrome in the horn tank, fenders, even the housing for the rear reflector, emphasized that this was no ordinary bicycle.

In some ways, Schwinn was taking a page from the automobile industry, which had discontinued the everboxy Model T years ago and embarked on annual model changes. General Motors even had a corporate department called the Styling Section to determine the nature and extent of these changes. At Schwinn, new styles came out of meetings between Frank W., his engineers, and salesmen who brought reports in from the field. For bicycles, unlike cars, the process was informal, but the message in the late 1940s was unmistakable. The public was weary of the drab, standardized products that were available during the war. Consumers—and this included young ones—were demanding excitement.

The success of the Black Phantom, and other Phantoms that were red and green, was not hard to fathom. From the moment they arrived on the dealers' showrooms, youngsters viewed their sleek lines and screaming chrome as the closest thing they could get, at the moment anyhow, to a vehicle with a motor. Big, substantial, and expensive-looking, Phantoms even had a taillight equipped with a feature that made it flash brightly upon the slightest touch of the coaster brake.

Not everyone who wanted a Black Phantom got one, which was probably part of the allure. In Grelton, Ohio, Larry Bush was a high school freshman in 1952 when he was ready for a good new bicycle. Bush—now a collector and classic-bike dealer—knew about Black Phantoms, and also knew their price, already up from the original $59.95. The Phantom was advertised in the popular comic books of the day where its up-to-date features were illustrated in full color.

Unfortunately, Bush didn't live near a Schwinn dealer and couldn't quite cover the price of the high-end Schwinn anyway. Instead, he got a ride to nearby Napoleon, Ohio, walked into the local hardware store, and rolled out with a Hiawatha balloon-tire model which he rode home. (Two years later, Bush had mowed

enough lawns and baled enough hay to afford a Black Phantom, but by this time his tastes had changed and he put his money into a used Whizzer.)

Another bicycle story with a different outcome involved a youngster named Wes Pinchot, who grew up to become a bicycle collector and owner of several Phantoms after the model had become a classic and was priced in the thousands. Pinchot lived on Chicago's North Side, and in 1948 was the winner of a Schwinn B-6 in the kind of promotion that Schwinn dealers were conducting in neighborhoods throughout the country. The free bicycle went to Pinchot whose name was drawn among hundreds of entry blanks dropped in a box at the local theater. At intermission of a Saturday matinee, young Wes came away with his first new bike.

The Schwinn B-6 was a desirable piece of machinery at this time, with a cantilever frame and even a brake light. Pinchot was more than pleased as he rode around his neighborhood. Unfortunately, he did not always take advantage of another patented feature of the Schwinn, the Cycelock, and one afternoon outside a dime store his prize bicycle was stolen. This being a different era from our own, the theft was worthy of a small article in a local weekly newspaper, and a nearby cigar store owner thought he might get some publicity for himself by a simple bit of goodwill. He replaced Pinchot's bike, buying him a J.C. Higgins from Sears (once, but no longer a Schwinn customer), an act that was duly reported in the paper.

Opposite

Schwinn was fully tooled up for the baby boom by 1949 when the Panther was supplying the enormous demand for balloon-tire models.

With soldiers coming home from Europe where bicycles were indispensable, Schwinn hoped to generate a postwar boom in lightweights. The Traveler was economical, but it was up against the a flood of cheaper imports from war-torn France and England.

The 1950 Panther had all the most desirable Schwinn features, like a spring fork and ample chrome, but lacked the cantilever frame. Though the Panther's streamed lines were considered racy and ultramodern, according to brochures, true connoisseurs knew that your parents had to spend a bit more for the ultimate, which was, of course, the Black Phantom.

Pinchot was grateful but never quite happy with his chain-store bike. He rode it happily enough, but a year or so later he walked into his local bicycle shop—Abt Cycle near Wrigley Field—and made a proposal. He badly wanted a Phantom and offered his J.C. Higgins in trade; he could pay the difference in installments, to be worked off through menial chores at the shop. The proposal was accepted, the only question being that of color; Pinchot felt he was beyond a mere Black Phantom. He opted for a red one, less common in most areas and a status symbol par excellence in his neighborhood. Pinchot rode the Schwinn for several years until it went the way of most balloon-tire bicy-

cles—languishing in the family garage and eventually hauled away by the junk dealer.

Wes Pinchot later entered the field of architecture, but when he was old enough to wax nostalgic for his youth, he became a collector of old bicycles, eventually locating, buying, and restoring a number of old Phantoms. While collecting grew popular in the 1980s, Pinchot took the hobby more seriously than most, and he acquired sufficient restoring skill to become the nationally advertised "Fender Doctor." His work in repairing outlandishly expensive parts for classic bicycles turned into a business and a labor of love—traceable, of course, to the major acquisition and indisputable high point of his youth.

Hands-On Marketing

Schwinn was having notable success when Ray Burch was lured from the failing Whizzer Motor Co. the year after the Black Phantom was introduced. Still, when Burch was hired as sales promotions manager, Frank W. made it clear that his job was to bring increased method to Schwinn's marketing department. Burch began by developing a more cohesive sales network, as he had previously done at Whizzer. For Schwinn, he traveled incessantly and became intimately acquainted with distributors and retailers. Later as marketing vice president, he never stopped traveling and became a hands-on vice president if there ever was one.

One of the first things Burch did when he arrived at Schwinn in 1950 was to examine the company's dealer list. He was astonished to find 15,000 names on it. A closer look revealed, predictably, that the majority of the so-called retailers were "independent," but they were not bicycle shops at all. Many were small hardware stores, dime stores, and more than a few were the least promising of outlets—barber shops, taverns, and the like. Many of these "retailers" might have sold a bike now and then and were still getting mailings and maybe an occasional visit from a bewildered Schwinn representative.

In 1950, Arnold, Schwinn & Co. was still making Paramounts for the track, and still producing a touring bicycle of the same name. Both were works of bicycle art but a long way from profitability.

The 1951 Starlet had color and pizzazz. Its popularity suggested that girl's weren't obsessed with the chrome and streamlining that boys were demanding from their bicycles in the Black Phantom era.

Rim mills, a rarity in American bike factories, were an important part of the operation at Schwinn. Ultimately, they enabled Frank Schwinn to specify the 1 3/4-inch rim as ideal for the middleweight.

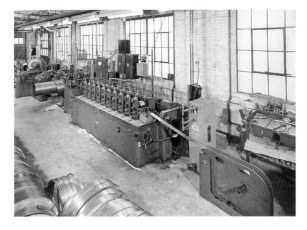

In 1954, the Schwinn middleweight was introduced, starring the Corvette, named after Chevrolet's sports car. Third from left is marketing man Ray Burch, sixth from left is Frank V. Schwinn, and standing at right is Edward R. Schwinn, who was known more for driving a Corvette than riding one.

This was not the best way to run a bicycle company, Burch concluded, and he resolved to find out for himself the difference between a true independent bicycle dealer and the others. One of his more telling visits came in the early 1950s on his way back from Florida where he had been meeting with wholesalers and with Frank W. at his winter home. In Indianapolis, he stopped in at one of the hardware stores on the Schwinn retailer list.

"I'd like to see some bicycles," Burch said without identifying himself to the man at the cash register.

"We have some," said the man who turned out to be the owner.

"I don't see any," Burch said.

"They're in back." The two walked to a dark back room, and the owner snapped a dust rag at one of the three lonely balloon-tire bicycles.

"Those are old models," Burch said.

"Old but never ridden," the hardware man said. "Truth is, we don't get much call for bicycles in here."

At this point Burch nodded and pulled out one of his calling cards. As he introduced himself he said, "I don't think we'll be bothering you with any more bicycles for a while." Not every dealer got such a personal treatment, but little by little, Burch was determined to get some control over the retail organization.

Even though the country was in the midst of an enormous postwar economic boom, and even though Schwinn was having astounding success with Phantoms and several other models, Burch always saw room for improvement. The competition—including Murray Ohio and Huffman which continued to turn in larger numbers than Schwinn—offered lower prices and was doing big business with chain stores. Schwinn, it was generally recognized, had a superior product, and though it had some very good dealers, Burch believed the company could do better with a more exclusive arrangement. It was the beginning of the "authorized dealer" network.

Other eye-openers came in the next year or so, and some were unexpected. At the prestigious department store, Marshall Field & Co. in Chicago, employees were famously skilled at selling a whole range of products from lace and china to appliances and books. But in bicycles, Burch found, they were bunglers. Sales staff had little idea how to "fit" a bicycle to a child and often sold one too big. "Let him grow into it," they said. Certainly, Field's was not alone in misunderstanding how to sell and service a bike. Complaints were coming into the Schwinn office in a steady stream.

Burch had another unpleasant but instructive experience during a trip to New Orleans where a local dealer was having good sales, but whose shop was less than pristine. Burch held his tongue during most of his visit, wondering what he could do to encourage the dealer to display bicycles in a more exemplary fashion. Then in the back room, Burch saw a bucketful of used three-speed hubs.

"What's that," Burch asked.

"Defective hubs," the dealer said.

"What's wrong with them?"

"I wish I knew," the dealer said smiling.

After a few more questions, Burch discovered that the dealer hadn't the foggiest idea how an internal-gear hub was serviced. The problem with each one, it turned out, could have been fixed by adjusting a small screw. Instead, the dealer cut the "defective" ones out and replaced them.

Burch did not rush to terminate dealers; Frank W. was conservative on this point. Still, it was apparent that 90 percent of Schwinn's volume was sold by 15 percent of its retail dealers. And despite what the company stressed, which was independent and knowledgeable dealers, it was clear that only a minority of them really measured up. By the mid-1950s, Burch and the Schwinn marketing staff made it their business to find out more about the ones that did.

The Total-Concept Store

The brightest star among Schwinn's independent bicycle dealers at the time was a former Marine named George Garner, owner of several bicycle shops outside

The 1954 Jaguar was a deluxe balloon-tire bike designed for the youngster who dreamed of speed but still crashed his bike into curbs. It was not quite a Phantom, but among Panthers, Hornets, and Tigers, this one was near the top.

Many Hollywood stars in the '40s found that a spin on a bicycle gave their image a down-to-earth touch, and that they made Schwinns not just desirable, but glamorous.

Discharged from the Marines after a wartime tour in the Pacific, he began to work for Hans Ohrt who had already established himself as one of the nation's leading promoters of adult cycling. Ohrt had a pair of shops in North Hollywood and Beverly Hills, and in trendsetting California he developed a following. Nothing was more healthful and efficient than cycling, he wrote in trade magazines and occasional newspaper articles. He noted especially that while most men already knew how to ride a two wheeler, it was women who could really benefit. "The good reward goes to the legs and hips," Ohrt declared without embarrassment.

Ohrt sold many different brands, including imports, but he liked the Schwinn lightweights. So did a healthy number of movie stars, as it turned out, many of whom became good customers of Ohrt's shops. The fact that Jane Russell, Bing Crosby, and Frank Sinatra were sometimes seen in Ohrt's stores did nothing to harm the image of a pastime that was previously regarded by most people as child's play.

High-profile clientele led to another marketing opportunity, celebrity endorsements. Hans Ohrt suggested it to some of his famous customers, and the campaign got off the ground just before World War II when Los Angeles wholesaler Bob Wilson, a boating and social pal of many members of the film crowd, got a number of stars to pose for Schwinn advertising photos. The campaign continued through the 1940s for surprisingly little cost—mostly studio publicity and a free bicycle. (Ronald Reagan wrote into his agreement that the bicycle in his photograph would be his.)

Garner believed in the potential of the bicycle, particularly as he noticed the growth of the L.A.W. in California. He decided that a growing market could be tapped if other stores besides Ohrt's did their part in promoting cycling as a wholesome activity. Garner also noted that the average bicycle shop in the 1940s remained in the back alley—a soot-filled establishment and not the kind of place where most families felt comfortable. What he imagined was a highly polished retail establishment.

Garner bought Valley Cyclery in Van Nuys, California, in April, 1947, with mostly borrowed money. When he got it, the shop was only partly for bicycles; hobbies and lawnmower sharpening were also stock in trade. But it wasn't long before Garner lost patience with those sidelines, and he could hardly help himself one day when a youngster walked in and asked him how much for a balsa wood airplane kit. Garner looked at him and nearly snarled, "You want it? It's yours." Within a few days nearly every boy in Van Nuys paid Valley Cyclery a visit, and while free airplane models quickly ran out, many of the kids became regular customers when the store sold nothing but bikes.

Los Angeles. Garner had been a bicycle racer before World War II when the sport was exotic and relatively unknown. He was not a standout in competition, but he loved bicycles and could see that there was a future in the business, especially in California. Garner decided to get into it.

The Fully Equipped Schwinn!
World Traveler !

"Gee, Schwinn Lightweights feel light as a
feather and ride like the breeze! And
they're American made, too!"

For Sport...Utility...or Touring!

For those who want a fine lightweight bicycle, fully equipped with all the
popular accessories. Schwinn caliper hand brakes, famous three-speed Sturmey-
Archer rear hub, self-generating electric headlight, and roomy saddle bag.
Schwinn Exclusive Quality Features throughout in smart styling. Made in
America so you know it's the best, with service readily available.
26 inch adult size model No. W-18.
24 inch boys' size model No. W-25.

The Schwinn World Traveler for Girls.
The same quality features and many popular accessories
in the girl's New World Traveler. Its light weight makes it
so easy to pedal, and the three-speed gearshift just eats
up the hills. 26 inch model No. W-68.

Three speed hubs, derailleur,
and the famous Sturmey-
Archer hub are available.

Lighting sets are a
necessity for night
riding. All of the w
known makes will fi
your Schwinn.

By the early 1950s, new lines of
lightweights were added to the Schwinn
catalogue, now with a big emphasis on
the three-speed internal-gear hub made
in England by Sturmey-Archer. The
New World became the World Traveler,
soon to become one of the best names
in touring bikes, the Traveler.

If Garner's model-kit promotion was spontaneous,
there was nothing haphazard about his approach to selling
bicycles. Inventory—he soon had exclusively Schwinns—
was lined up neatly in the showroom. Salesmen were
trained. They knew the workings of the machine, and the
mechanics (often doubling as salesmen) knew that they'd
all sell more bicycles if they wore clean aprons and spoke
patiently with customers. The approach worked marvelously, and within a few years, George Garner opened
four more shops in the Los Angeles area.

As Schwinn volume in Southern California grew,
Ray Burch kept steady contact with Garner. Then in

1952 Paramount Tourist. The best-built bicycle in America—maybe the whole world—could be outfitted and painted very much to the taste of the owner. The owner in this case was Frank W. Schwinn who preferred green paint, upright handlebars, a three-speed internal-gear rear hub, and the finest lugs that money could buy.

1956, he decided to spend some time at one of Garner's locations, witness his sales technique, and devise a way to teach it to other Schwinn dealers nationwide. Burch brought a tape recorder with him for the visit so he wouldn't miss a word. Accompanied by Frank V. Schwinn, Frank W.'s son and soon to be president of Arnold, Schwinn & Co., they set it up in Garner's store and waited.

What they discovered was unexpected. The sales talk was relatively brief. It was a short description, usually directed to a father, of mechanical features of the given model, usually interrupted by the youngster who broke in with his (usually a boy's) predictable pleas. Many sales points were unspoken. Judging from the store, the bicycle itself was assumed to be of high quality. The shop clearly provided service (especially compared to other retailers where it was nonexistent). Quickly and with minimal discussion, the sale was 90 percent made.

"How much is this bicycle," the father would ask. Told that it was $79.95, which was then the price of a Phantom, he said, "That's a lot of money for a bicycle." In reply, the salesman—often Garner himself—said little. The buyer looked around at the splendid displays and the well-dressed mechanics, then at his dewy-eyed son. There was little left to talk about.

With Garner's advice and counsel, Burch and other members of the Schwinn marketing staff developed a new kind of bicycle shop. The "total-concept store," as they called it, involved the most eye-catching displays and a repair shop in full view. It involved getting rid of the "riff-raff" dealers who were unable to spend proper dollars to raise their image. It also meant neon signs for Schwinn shops, some of them 10-feet high for outside the store, and other "silent salesmen" in posters and displays inside. Schwinn was putting its fate in the hands of its dealers, and vice versa. This motivated increased national advertising notably in *Life* magazine—that really made dealers stock up, said Burch. Eventually, a National Service School was traveling to Holiday Inns all over the country, making sure that all dealers could service and sell with uniform skill. Selling Schwinns, Burch and "Frankie" V. Schwinn now decided, was going to be a first-class operation, not to mention a more expensive one.

The total-concept store was a refinement of what Frank W. had envisioned in the past, which was to sell via the best and most knowledgeable retailers possible. So in theory, the boss could hardly disagree with shortening and strengthening the list of retailers. In practice, however, it was harder to swallow. The turning point for Frank Schwinn came in the late 1950s, and the issue was B.F. Goodrich, which once sold a full 25 percent of Schwinn's volume in the early balloon-tire days

While B.F. Goodrich still posted respectable numbers, problems had been growing with the account for some time. They continued to discount Schwinns, only a few dollars but to the sharp irritation of other dealers who were told not to cut prices. (Fair trade laws that enforced the authorized retail price in most states were soon to come.) Goodrich, moreover, provided little if any service after the sale, and this was leading to customer complaints mailed to the Schwinn offices. Burch didn't like the Goodrich situation, and neither did Frankie. Before long, Frank W. was hearing about it regularly.

"I guess you're going to lose me that account," the older Schwinn said to the younger men. Frank W., who had

developed a close rapport with older Goodrich executives, would light a cigarette and smile thinly. Burch would tell him about Alfred P. Sloan of General Motors and his absolute dedication to the dealers. Frank W. could not argue as he knew as well as anyone that the company depended upon the most up-to-date retailers in the business.

Sales to B.F. Goodrich were discontinued, and what soon emerged was an early form of franchising, though Schwinn always called retailers "authorized dealers," with the implication that the company's

Comic books had been a Schwinn advertising staple since 1940. In the 1950s, the company produced its own, and in this issue, dated 1959, they put the girl's Starlet on the inside back cover.

Frank W. Schwinn at a sales meeting, circa 1957. He understood the engineering and marketing of bicycles with equal facility and made Schwinn the Chevrolet, Buick, and Cadillac of the American bike business all rolled into one.

authorization could be withdrawn at any time. By the 1960s, the number of authorized dealers was reduced to 2,000, and in 1968, Schwinn hit 1 million bicycles sold. (It had sold 510,000 in 1950.) Good economic times powered this growth, and the baby boom certainly was a major factor. But making Schwinn both the Cadillac and Chevrolet of the bicycle trade depended as much on *selling* a high-quality product as it did on making it.

European Invasion

The formula was successful but not easy. Over the course of the 1950s, for example, European competition was causing what many people called a "crisis in the American bike industry." The problem was tariffs, virtually nonexistent in the early postwar years. (Free traders in Washington were committed to supporting European industry to help wartime allies generate revenue to repay their oversized war debts.) Devaluation of the British Pound was another blow for American bicycles which in the 1950s were facing their toughest competition from one of the most prestigious names in cycling, Raleigh. This threat was less troublesome for Schwinn than most American bicycle makers, as Schwinn had been fighting low-price competition all along. Still, it required vigilance to make sure that authorized dealers were doing properly by the company, and when not, that they were terminated.

In the late 1950s, for example, Ray Burch visited a Schwinn dealer close to his home in suburban Chicago. Again incognito, he asked about lightweight bicycles, and specifically about Schwinn's three-speed Traveler. The
continued on page 105

1959 Wasp. In an era of middleweights, balloon-tire bicycles might have seemed passé, but the Wasp was the "heavy-duty model" of the Schwinn line. It featured old-fashioned balloon-tires and came with or without a spring fork—and took as much punishment per bicycle as any model that Schwinn produced.

By 1959 the Mark IV Jaguar had become "America's Middleweight Masterpiece" with three-speed gears, hand brakes, headlight, and two carriers. Red, blue, green, and black were available.

By the mid-1950s, Schwinn was promoting its now-famous name through "total concept stores," as authorized dealerships were called. Local bike shops were still family operations, but with advice, counsel, and signage from headquarters in Chicago, they were turned into professional, well-equipped establishments. These photos were made by the company to illustrate that the successful bike shop was a clean, well-lighted place.

By 1960, there was reason to believe that the adult market which had so vexed Frank W. Schwinn might begin to grow. Here, an advertising photo shows that the Corvette was not just suitable for curb-crunching, but also for gentle riding in the neighborhood.

continued from page 101

dealer was happy to describe the Schwinn, but then walked over to another section of the store where the imports were displayed. "Here's a Raleigh," the dealer said. "It's lighter and a few dollars cheaper, too." He even claimed the Raleigh had a better reputation, which was arguable, but what was absolutely clear was that the markup on European bikes was almost always higher, and this dealer was pushing customers in that direction for that reason.

Burch understood the tactic well enough. Advertising Schwinns got customers in the door, but they could be induced to buy a Raleigh with a little nudge. This situation was an unhappy one for Burch. It was unhappy for the dealer, too, when Burch pulled out one of his cards. "We won't be sending you any more bicycles for a while," the Schwinn vice president said as he left.

The Rise of the Middleweights

The natural objective of Schwinn's marketing department was to convince selected bicycle shops to sell Schwinns and nothing but Schwinns. There were many ways to induce loyalty, but nothing worked like having a full line of products for the dealer to sell. That was the idea behind the Schwinn line of "middleweight" bicycles, which were introduced in 1954.

It was no flash of brilliance that inspired the development of middleweights—the Corvette, the Jaguar, the Panther, and a number of others. The postwar influx of European lightweights had created a fashion for lighter bikes among some kids, and it was apparent to several engineers at the company that they could do well if they produced something with the durability of a balloon-tire model and the ridability of a lightweight. Around 1952, Frank W. encouraged the engineers, whose offices were just a flight of stairs down from the "Old Man" as Frank W. was now called, to pursue it. So engineering manager Bill Jacoby, a former six-day rider, began assembling the parts—fork, rims, and tires for a 1 5/8-inch wheel—mostly from a supplier who sent them from Europe. Frame makers also worked up something that was flash-welded and cantilever-framed, not too different from the balloon-tire models that served so well.

When he saw the first prototype, Frank W. seemed less than enthusiastic about middleweights. Reasons were not hard to fathom. The Black Phantom was a phenomenal success at the time, and Schwinn had nearly a quarter of the American bike market. Some wondered how much better the company could do. The middleweight idea languished for a while, but by early 1954, the three-speed, hand-braked Corvette was in production along with coaster-brake middleweights as well. No one ever knew what motivated Frank W. to move on the middleweight idea—he was inscrutable as he was autocratic—but he eventually turned out sketches of his own, and the line was in the stores a few months later. Whatever else overcame the boss's resistance, Schwinn's middleweight featured non-standard 1 3/4-inch wheels—requiring new rims from Schwinn rim mills and new molds for the tires.

Public response to the middleweight line was almost immediate. More often than not, the new Schwinns satisfied kids who otherwise had speedy but fragile European bikes on their mind. Parents, meanwhile, were concerned with the durability issue.

"Parents are usually easy to talk into a middleweight," said Gary Kerwer, a Chicago dealer, at the time. "But the kids have to be sold. . . . We ask the kids if any of their friends ride lightweights, and they always say 'yes.' Then we ask them if they noticed how much they were in the repair shop. That's about all it takes to make the sale."

Dealers found that solid-built middleweights rode better than most lightweights anyway, at least for kids accustomed to balloon-tire bikes. They were more than a happy medium between two extremes. A Corvette—cleverly named after Chevrolet's sports car introduced in 1953—became a very big deal in many neighborhoods, and that was all it took for middleweight sales to double in 1955 and to lead all lines by the following year.

Captain Kangaroo not only promoted Schwinn on television, he often attended meetings and shows on behalf of America's favorite bicycle. Here with the grandchildren of Frank W. Schwinn, two future Schwinn executives get some marketing pointers from a master. Edward, Jr. is standing beside the Captain and Richard is on the bike.

Chapter Eight

THE NEW BICYCLE BOOM

MAKE IT A Schwinn CHRISTMAS

bike prices include complete assembly

Chicago, once America's great bicycle capital during the boom of the 1890s, remained a center of the industry, but in the 1960s it was due almost entirely to the fact that Schwinn was located there.

Chicago had its benefits, as a shipping center and reliable source of labor. But there were also disadvantages. One was that it was not Europe, where the most advanced cycling trends were taking place, and also that it was not California which was now the birthplace of several crucial turning points in the development of the American bicycle.

By the mid-1950s, the market had outgrown the big balloon-tire bike, and the middleweight would soon go into eclipse as well. The next major trend in bicycles was already evolving; executives at Schwinn called it "speed bikes." Equipped with an exotic European invention, the derailleur, bicycles would soon be known as "ten speeds" (some early ones in this country had eight gears). Imported speed bikes began to emerge in small pockets in California—where Schwinn was fortunate to have good dealers who were quick to point out to Schwinn management in Chicago that a new phenomenon was about to begin.

Actually, the ten-speed story went back to just after World War II when derailleur-gear bicycles with drop handlebars were rare but not unknown. The blue-collar sport of track racing was fading on the few velodromes left in America. But road racing, a fervent national pastime in some countries of Europe, was being encouraged by a few bicycle dealers around the country and particularly in the San Francisco area. For those interested in a unique new sport, imported lightweights with derailleur gears were available and attracted a few devoted enthusiasts.

One of the early road racers of the period was a teenager named George Koenig, son of a German-immigrant professor at Stanford University. Hanging out at the Palo Alto Bicycle Shop, Koenig got his first road racer, a French-made Automoto with a four-gear freewheel. Sometimes he convinced friends to join him on rides, often long and hard in the mountains on the peninsula. But usually he worked out by himself on lonely roads, and it was during one such afternoon that he met another rider doing the same thing. His name was Rick Bronson.

The two became fast friends, and Bronson soon insisted they travel that summer to Europe and race on the junior circuit in Italy. It was not hard to get Koenig to agree, so they bought tickets and were successful in joining up with a number of junior racing clubs in Milan, Rome, and many other cities in between. It was the greatest summer vacation ever for both of them, and when they returned home in the fall, they did what they could to make sure it would never end. With several friends they formed a club of their own, the *Pedali Alpini* (the "Alpine Cyclists" in Italian), and spent most of their free time training.

In the late 1950s, the teenage *Pedali* lived, breathed, and ate bicycles, and Bronson seemed to be the most possessed. He insisted that the only proper carbohydrates were in pasta. He named his dog Fausto after the great Italian cyclist Fausto Coppi. And he bewildered his parents by discarding his rock and roll

Left
The Varsity, Schwinn's biggest seller in the bike boom that began in the late 1960s, introduced a generation of young riders to touring cycles.

Above
By the late 1960s, the ideal family was showing up everywhere. Schwinn weighed in with their own version—mother and father on ten speeds and the kids on Sting-Rays and Krates.

Introduced in June 1960, the Varsity had eight speeds with the front derailleur shifted by direct lever on the seat post. The Varsity required some changes in subsequent years to get it just right—and it was always a bit heavy—but more than any other American bicycle it introduced millions of youngsters to road bikes and became one of the most famous models in American cycling.

In 1967, Schwinn introduced the Twin-Stik attached beneath the stem. It was the result of a collaboration between Schwinn and the Japanese component maker Shimano, a relationship that would last for years.

records and playing Italian opera in his room at night. Whether Bronson's love of things Italian made him a better cyclist is an open question, but his enthusiasm was contagious, and the *Pedali* traveled as a group all over California and entered races where they could find them.

Other road-racing clubs were being formed at the time as well, and the sport's popularity was on the rise. While it's again doubtful that the often-strange behavior of the *Pedali* was behind this surge in interest, Bronson and Koenig (who would sometimes speak to each other in Italian) certainly made an impression on the growing number of cyclists on the West Coast at the time. Their story was later told to a Los Angeles screenwriter who included more than a few details about the teenagers in the movie *Breaking Away*.

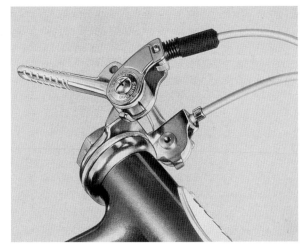

Schwinn did nothing to jump on this trend in the late 1950s. Lightweights were still selling slowly for the company. Three-speeds had grown modestly in the 1950s, but any executive who mentioned speed bikes in that period was reminded of a dismal experiment a few years before. The company sent to Europe for 1,000 derailleur sets and put them on lightweight frames. This result did not surprise old Frank W., of course. These eight-speeds, called Continentals, failed to achieve even middling success in the stores. Everyone agreed that it was a well-built flash-welded machine. Though it was hardly feathery in weight, that wasn't the problem. Quite simply, most of Schwinn's good dealers at the time were family-oriented retailers. They had little knack for selling a new product for someone to jump aboard, tuck his

head low to the handlebars, and scorch past smiling kids on Black Phantoms and Corvettes.

Another reason for the failure of Schwinn's early experiment with road racers rested in the mind-set of the company. Schwinn's postwar growth came primarily through the efforts of the marketing executives—at least that was how most people inside the company viewed it. An early derailleur concept clearly came from the factory, the domain of Edward Schwinn, Frankie's younger brother. Nothing like hostility marked relations between the people who manufactured Schwinns and the people who marketed them. But people with power in the company never put sales muscle behind the unfortunate eight speed. The result was that almost all of them sat in the warehouse until 1958 when the model was discon-

1961 Corvette. The right formula for derailleur bikes in the early 1960s was not obvious. A five-speed middleweight was a possibility and was sold for a while before being quickly overshadowed by the ten-speed Continental and Varsity.

In the 1960s, the old flash-welding technology was considered the envy of the industry. But soon it would be something of an albatross when less hefty lug-frame bikes of lighter steels, unsuitable to the process of "electronically forged" frames, became the rage.

Schwinn
ELECTRONICALLY FORGED FRAME

SCHWINN BIKES DO RIDE NOTICEABLY BETTER, THEY DO "STAND UP!" THEY DON'T "FALL APART."

Schwinn Frame Head Extra Strength Only on Schwinn

Rear Fork Ends Stronger, Welded on

Crank Hanger Exclusive Extra Strength Design

Built-in Kickstand Welded on, Rattle-Free

...STRONGEST MADE!

1964 Super Deluxe Sting-Ray. Restored by W.D. Durham with parts from an Arizona specialty supplier called Hyper-Formance, it has a two-speed kickback rear hub, a Sting-Ray headlamp, a factory-spec windshield, and many other features coveted by growing numbers of collectors.

tinued. Derailleur sets were scrapped and the frames were re-equipped as standard lightweights.

Fortunately, some people at Schwinn kept their eye on the speed-bike market. Frank W., for one, almost inexplicably kept a soft spot in his heart for racing, even donating the lavish Ignaz Schwinn Trophy for the all-around championship of the National Bicycle League of America between 1946 and 1949. The company also continued to build Paramounts, still the best stock racing bicycle built in America. And for various reasons, he hired a number of bicycle racers for important jobs at Schwinn.

Among these racers, the most notable was a 1952 Olympian, Frank Brilando, who later became vice president of engineering. Brilando quit active racing shortly after he joined the company but kept his hand in the sport. When the 1959 Pan American Games were held in Chicago, for example, Brilando helped organize the bicycle-racing events. He also designed the wooden track and

coached the four-man 4,000-meter pursuit team that won the gold medal—the first international win for U.S. cyclists in decades. Between Frank W. and Brilando, racing bicycles maintained a presence at Schwinn despite the fact that it was anything but profitable. Most of the American team at the Pan Am Games was riding Paramounts (or a Wastyn-made racer that was almost indistinguishable). The following year, a number of those same athletes competed in the Olympics at Rome, where Paramounts (including a racing tandem) were used in road and track events.

Then in 1960, as racing and touring in the sunny climes of California were making a perceptible mark in bicycle shops around the state, Schwinn's Los Angeles wholesaler Bob Wilson, president of Harry Wilson Bicycle Sales, called Al Fritz, vice president of Schwinn. Speed bikes with derailleur gears were selling out, he said. If Schwinn could produce something like them, they could easily have part of this market themselves. Fritz, remem-

Right, Below and Opposite
1968–1973 Krate series. The design was ingenious. The forward lean of the Krate resembled drag racers, and the smaller wheel enabled engineers to use old tooling for the spring fork that had gone on old Phantoms. The stick-shift caused some safety concerns, but that was nothing for young riders who braved the streets of suburban neighborhoods and the dirt on vacant lots. The Krate became a national icon and remains one of the great classic bikes of its era.

bering the derailleur experiment, was pessimistic, but Wilson promised a good first order. So Fritz brought the proposal to Frank W. and Frankie Schwinn. They approved the new model, and late that year, a new Continental eight speed was introduced. It had a flash-welded frame, but featured a tubular fork, aluminum handlebars, and other components designed for lightness. Within a year, and with sales coming at a good clip, Schwinn came out with the Varsity, a slightly less expensive version equipped with steel bars and a forged front fork.

The Varsity Boom

With two new models, Schwinn primed the derailleur market, which would need several more years to surge. Before that happened, Brilando and Al Fritz continued making improvements in ten speeds, and while the Varsity remained heavy as far as "lightweights" went, it was refined as a durable and easy-to-ride Schwinn well before the bicycle boom of the late 1960s, which made all previous bicycle booms look like tag sales.

One of the early problems with the Varsity was the manner in which the derailleurs were controlled. The lever for the rear was low on the downbar and the front derailleur was moved by direct linkage (no cable at all) and required a long and even dangerous reach. (Levers were later placed on the stem, though this irritated

purits.) Another problem was in the rear sprockets and freewheel. Originally imported from Europe, their initial design was usually fine for clear paved roads where old-time racers rode in places like France and Italy. But when American kids got their hands on them and rode them over hill and dale, not to mention sandlots, the bearings in freewheels got filled with dirt and grit. This did not usually effect performance, but it could be noisy.

Al Frtiz discussed this shortcoming with his European suppliers, and while nodding sympathetically they were notably unresponsive on the subject. Schwinn ordered free-wheels from at least two different makers in the early years, but the problem persisted. In the meantime, Fritz had been having pleasant conversations with Keizo Shimano, the middle brother of a family-owned component company in Japan. At industry conferences, Shimano was always there, tireless in seeking out Fritz and other American bicycle executives. Eager for Schwinn business, Shimano asked Fritz what problems they were having with current suppliers and how he might help to solve them. It was on a golf course in Florida where the two spoke in earnest about the freewheel problems on the Varsity.

In the early 1960s, the aerospace industry was a big design influence for other bike makers. Schwinn came up with this unbuilt design, but the company had all it could handle at the time with the 10-speed and Sting-Ray manias.

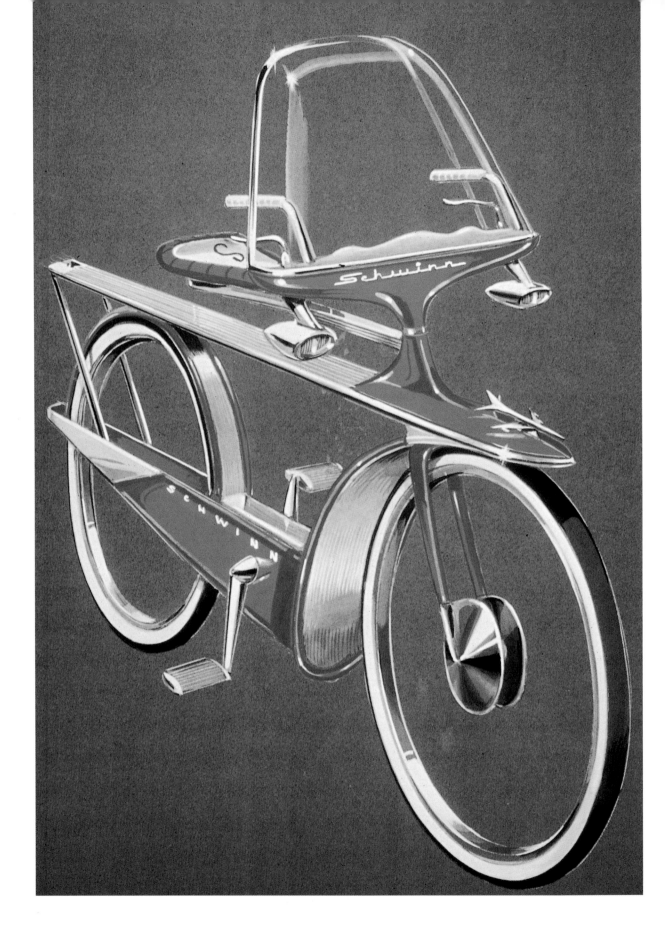

In the bicycle boom that began in 1969, Schwinn worked hard to spread its popularity beyond the big-selling Varsitys and Krates. Adults could ride without sacrificing comfort or anything else that went into having a good time, while gas-guzzling autos were for dinosaurs.

Krates had been on the market for two years when the fifth addition to the line, the Cotton Picker, was introduced in the 1970 catalogue. Bucket seats were deeper and roomier, and handlebars were narrower and sportier.

Within three months, Shimano had something to show the people in Chicago: a freewheel with a sealed bearing. The Shimano freewheel worked well, Schwinn engineers liked it, and a substantial order was placed. It was not only a needed refinement for Schwinn's ten-speed, but also Shimano's first major success in this country—to be repeated, of course—and marked the Japanese firm as a first-class supplier of the American bicycle industry.

"Pig Bikes"

The Varsity pointed to the beginning of demographic change in the bicycle-riding public. Adolescents took to Varsitys by the thousands, and they would eventually shift to still-lighter and more expensive road bikes. But before that happened, an enormous movement of a different kind came about in American bicy-cles. This one was based on the old rules of the business—which meant kids buy-ing bicycles that reminded them of things with engines.

Schwinn noticed the potential for a totally new style of bicycle in late 1962 when one of the company's traveling representatives took Al Fritz aside at a meeting. "Something goofy" was happening in California, the rep said. Retailers could not keep 20-inch frames in stock, and even second-hand 20 inchers were getting bought up as soon as they showed up in shops. The fad was something kids called "pig bikes"—refitting small frames

1975 Town and Country. A sure sign that bicycles were not just fashionable but useful too was that the older set took to them, sometimes the three-wheeled variety with a basket in back large enough for a family-sized load of groceries.

with "longhorn" handlebars and something called "polo seats." It became a craze in Orange County, where neighborhood fashions soon spread like fire on a dry hillside.

Fritz, who was formerly Frank W.'s secretary and first to see the Old Man's ideas when he drew them, was always open to something new. He asked his West Coast sales manager to send some longhorn bars. He also remembered an old polo seat that Robert Persons, of saddle maker Persons-Majestic, had tried to sell Schwinn some years before. Persons suggested it might work on a tandem of some sort, which was an idea that never got off the ground, but Fritz pushed some boxes around in a back room and found the samples.

When Fritz assembled what would become the classic Schwinn Sting-Ray, he was amazed and pleased. Even an adult could ride it with ease. It turned corners on a dime. There was even the feeling, untested by Fritz, that the bike could do a trick something like what popular drag racers were doing at the time: wheelstands.

Schwinn's lead time on products was never long—a bike could go from concept to market in just a few months. In this case, however, there was something else on everyone's mind, and that was the health of Frank W. who had been diagnosed with cancer that winter. When he died in April, 1963, it sent a shock through the industry, and his funeral at Chicago's Holy Name Cathedral brought bicycle people from all over the world. Burial was on a Friday, and afterward Fritz took three of his best wholesaler-distributors back to the office for quiet talks. Sometime during that *continued on page 120*

CAPTAIN KANGAROO ALWAYS SAYS, "Schwinn BIKES ARE BEST"

SCHWINN FRAME
Electronically forged. Tough and resilient for a lively ride — and it's the strongest made!

FORGED FRONT FORK
Tougher, absorbs road shock better than ordinary tubular forks.

TUBULAR RIMS
Extra-strength double-thickness tubular steel rims, five times more resistant to twist.

QUALITY EQUIPMENT
Compare the hubs, pedals, handlebars and grips, saddle, tires and tubes, and controls — all Schwinn quality.

BUILT-IN KICKSTANDS
Heavy-duty, welded-on, rattle-resistant kickstands — not just clamped on.

SOLD ONLY THROUGH . . .
Factory-trained franchised sales and service Schwinn Dealers. Every Schwinn Bike bears the Schwinn name plate. We make no private brands.

© 1969 ROBERT KEESHAN ASSOCIATES, INC.

RIDES BETTER...LASTS LONGER...COSTS LESS IN THE LONG RUN!

In 1969, Captain Kangaroo was still a leading spokesman for anyone wanting to reach youngsters with ideas about moving up, in this case to a lightweight Racer.

As Schwinn grew, the stakes were higher and the marketing more intense. During the bike boom that began in the late 1960s, Schwinn advertising pushed bicycles at times of year when sales otherwise tended to sag compared to the spring and summer.

Schwinn®
FIRST CHOICE FOR BACK-TO-SCHOOL

1975 Suburban. As Schwinn sought the adult cyclist, they put upright bars and padded seat on a Varsity frame and advertised the big-selling Suburban in *Reader's Digest*.

Right
Manta Rays had 24-inch wheels, not bad for bigger kids but never quite the ticket in neighborhoods where Sting-Rays and Krates had already become classics to the grade school set.

Schwinn was always conscious of the adult market, and the three-wheeler was a successful effort to show them that kids were not the only riders for a Schwinn. This tri-wheeler was prototyped in 1980, but the bike that made a hit among the retiring set was the larger-wheeled trike, the Town and Country.

continued from page 116
afternoon, Fritz took them up to the engineering department where he had his pig-bike prototype. All three bicycle men scoffed—that was until they rode it down an aisle in the paint room. For easy pedaling, tight corners, and just plain fun, they quickly agreed that this one seemed like a winner.

Finding names for new bicycles was one of Al Fritz's favorite jobs. He often perused the dictionary for agreeable word combinations, and when he came to an entry for "stingray," and saw a picture of the creature with wing-like fins, it was a natural. The fact that Chevrolet's Corvette

In 1970, the height of the bike boom was making bicycle dealers everywhere very happy indeed, and authorized Schwinn dealers were particularly pleased by the excellent attention they were getting from Chicago and several lines of bicycles—including the Varsity and the Sting-Ray—that defined their class.

Sting Rays were a rage among sports car enthusiasts, and the dearest fantasy of millions of kids, did not hurt either.

Enthusiasm about the Schwinn Sting-Ray was not unanimous when it was ready to come out in late 1963. One morning, for example, Fritz was pulling a prototype out of the trunk of his car when Frankie Schwinn, then the president of the company, saw it. Schwinn said the bike looked like a clinker to him. Fritz disagreed and predicted right there that it would sell 25,000 copies by the end of the year. Fritz was wrong. By early 1964 it had sold 45,000, and numbers would have been higher if suppliers hadn't run out of 20-inch tires.

One-Stop Cycle Shopping!

Your Neighborhood Schwinn Franchised Dealer

Exciting new accessories make cycling more fun. Your Franchised Schwinn Dealer offers a huge selection of everything that is new bicycle parts, accessories and supplies.

Your Franchised Schwinn Dealer is not just a limited department—but a whole store filled with a complete selection of new Schwinn bikes in every style, color, size and price.

Headquarters for the young in heart!

There's no thrill like a new bike! For the growing boy or girl, that new bike is the first feeling of really growing up—and for the grown-up it's a feeling of youth and first choice for physical fitness. Whatever your age, shape, taste or interest your nearby Schwinn Franchised Dealer is your one spot to shop for your new bike. Whether it's a trainer for junior or a sophisticated modern 10-speed for mom and dad, your Schwinn dealer can open the door to more fun. Stop in and discuss that thrill of the open road on a new Schwinn.

Making your cycling more fun is part of your dealer's job. Proper fit is important and no one knows more about bikes than your Schwinn man. When you buy a new Schwinn, it is assembled, adjusted, properly fitted and ready-to-ride —at no extra charge.

... and, if your new Schwinn ever needs service—there is a friendly reliable Schwinn Franchised Dealer to keep you riding carefree and secure.

Here's your nearby Schwinn dealer

SCHWINN BICYCLES SALES & SERVICE

reported in the school paper with the respect normally afforded football triumphs.

There was always something about Sting-Rays that made kids feel powerful—which might be partially behind the latter-day craze for collecting the bikes. In recent years, the leading collector's newsletter, *Sting-Ray City News* out of Scottsdale, Arizona, has always tried to capture some of that nostalgia, and in a 1995 article it reported the many nicknames for longhorn bars that were common around the country. In Chicago, for example, they called them "angle bars," and in Seattle they were "monkey bars."

Maybe the most intriguing handlebar story came out of Philadelphia where a group of kids used them in a way that was fortunately rather unique. They ground out the ends of the hand grips and filled the bars with go-cart fuel. The idea was to wait for a car to appear down the road, then one perpetrator would hold a cigarette lighter near one end, another would take a deep breath and blow hard in the other. The result was "a nice, straight, incredibly intense (and hot) wall of flame across the road," wrote one enthusiast who naturally had a name for handlebars used in this fashion: "flame throwers."

Schwinn executives back in Chicago never encouraged such dangerous activity. But they were definitely in tune with the wistful imaginations of kids. Through the 1960s, they introduced countless variations on the Sting-Ray. Manta-Rays were larger. Fastbacks had five-speed derailleurs in back and a big stick shift. The Krate series

Sports Illustrated spoke to the young adult market that Schwinn needed to attract in 1975—much of the lightweight market was already migrating to foreign-made bicycles. This ad came out in 1975 and emphasized that nothing was as American as riding a Schwinn.

Reader's Digest was another avenue to the adult market, and by 1978 the marketing department was putting its money and its faith in the Suburban, essentially a Varsity frame with five speeds, upright handlebars, and a padded seat.

Sting-Rays, or "high-rise" bicycles as they were called by the competition, captured the imagination of children everywhere, and they were versatile beyond Al Fritz's, or anyone else's, imagination. A girl on the back of the "banana seat," as Schwinn named it, became a mark of budding adolescence. Thousands of riders challenged off-road terrain, riding across vacant lots, even over dirt mounds on construction sites in suburbs all over America.

The antics that kids enjoyed on any bicycle were always the stuff of memories, but on Sting-Rays they simply could do more. The tricks that kids worked out on these models were not easily forgotten. Wheel-stands or "wheelies" were a command performance for anyone skillful enough to master them. As late as 1981, a high school junior in Murrysville, Pennsylvania, named Skip Richter accepted a challenge to ride his old Krate-series Sting-Ray five and a half miles on the rear wheel. A crowd from school was assembled to watch, and when Richter succeeded, the stunt was

1977 Paramount Tandem. This 15-speed model was an improvement over the 10-speed tandem of 1976. The step-through frame brought back something of the romantic days of the bicycle built for two, but only to an extent, as the curved rear seat post provided increased power in co-ed tandem riding.

1976 Sting-Ray and Fastback. Sting-Ray had bicentennial decals for the celebration, and the Fastback now featured a thumb-controlled five-speed derailleur. The stick shift on the top tube had been discouraged for safety reasons.

1979 World Sport. Lighter lug-frame bicycles were what the market wanted. Schwinn's flash-welding facility in Chicago could not build true lightweights like this one, so the company had this chrome-moly racer, like many other higher-end models, manufactured in Japan.

(with Orange Krates, Pea Pickers, and a number of others) were a direct inspiration from California drag strips.

Curiously, the Krates also had one foot in Schwinn's history. The spring front fork, a racy bit of hardware on a 20-inch Krate, was not too different from the once-innovative suspension system on old Phantoms. The Krate's smaller, 16-inch front wheel not only gave it the forward slope of a funny car, but also meant that Schwinn could make a spring fork that fit with tooling the factory already had, and it showed that Arnold, Schwinn & Co.'s design genius did not die with Frank W. Schwinn.

The L.A.W. Rises Again

The lightweight bicycle boom that began in the late 1960s was the result of many long-rumbling forces. One that

had been percolating for a long time was physical fitness. This movement got a strong push back in 1955 when President Eisenhower suffered a heart attack and the administration turned the President's cardiologist into a prominent government spokesman to calm the fears of the nation. That cardiologist, Dr. Paul Dudley White, was more than a competent and loquacious medical man. He was also an ardent cyclist, and White used his bully pulpit to promote bicycling as one of the most healthful things an adult could do.

Schwinn would be the major beneficiary of this national campaign, and the company did what it could to keep the momentum going. Most importantly, it took a bicycle salesman named Keith Kingbay out of the parts department, where he was languishing, and made him one of America's most tireless emissaries of cycling.

Even before Kingbay, who died in 1995 at the age of 80, was given the formal title of Schwinn's "bicycling activities manager," he talked about his passion for pedaling wherever he could. He was a member of the L.A.W. when it was revived for the short period in the 1940s, and in 1965 he was among still avid cyclists who discovered that the organization's old bank account was about to be turned over to the state for inactivity. Kingbay and several others decided to use what was left to celebrate the 25th anniversary of the lapsed Columbus Park chapter, and 250 people turned up. It was the beginning of the L.A.W.'s rebirth nationwide.

All through this period, Kingbay stayed on the cutting edge of promoting bicycles. When Mayor Richard J. Daley, always proud of Chicago's motto, "City in the Garden," decided that a bicycle path along the lakefront would enhance Chicago's reputation, Kingbay was in the center of it all. He helped bring Paul Dudley White in for the opening ceremonies.

Most of Keith Kingbay's efforts were absolutely grassroots. As the L.A.W. grew in the 1960s, "Mr. Bicycle," as he was called, spoke constantly to club chapters around the country. He described his own cycle tours around America and through Europe and even in South America. He always ended his talks—which advocated the sport at large more than any product made by Schwinn—with a favorite saying: "Bicycling, like youth, is too good to be wasted on the young."

Despite Kingbay's efforts among adults, however, the youth market remained Schwinn's strength, and it

1978 Hurricane 5. For kids whose fantasies hovered between motocross and the drag strip, the Hurricane was introduced in 1977 and had a "Positron II" shifting lever that made gears snap into position.

Bicycle touring was fashionable throughout the 1970s—as in this 1979 photo—though the more fashionable it became, the more cyclists were leaving their Varsitys and Continentals for fancier European makes.

There was little doubt about the juvenile bicycle of choice in 1980. This is a catalogue photo of the Sting-Ray Pixie and Convertible Lil' Tiger—the top tube was removable—at times when no one understood the kids' market better than Schwinn. The problem, of course, was that the kids that Schwinn understood were growing up and demanding bicycles that were distinctly unSchwinn-like.

was a mixed blessing. In the late 1950s, for example, the company staged an annual stock-bike race for youngsters at the old velodrome in Kenosha, Wisconsin. The teenager who won on his balloon-tire or middleweight bicycle was brought to Chicago and fitted for a Paramount. The idea, of course, was to generate publicity for adult lightweights. This it did, but the impact was naturally more on the kids than on their parents.

By the mid-1960s, as the Varsity and its slightly upscale brother, the Continental, were poised to change the bicycle business, Schwinn had overcome whatever resistance the market held toward derailleurs, partly through an ingenious in-store display device with cranks and derailleur mounted on a platform. Developed originally for use by the Schwinn Service School, it provided an exciting and easy-to-understand demonstration of ten speeds in the shops. Advertising was also successful at creating and capturing the Varsity's portion of the ten-speed market. *Boy's Life*, for example, was an economical media buy at the time, and cut straight into the age group that was ready for this kind of bike. The result of this and other promotions was that in 1971, when the

1982 Hollywood

1982 Typhoon

This Page and Next Two
In the late 1970s, the industry was in the throes of innovation. Schwinn understood the new bicycle market but could not respond as quickly as some makers, since it had millions of dollars tied up in the flash-welding equipment in its Chicago facility. Flash welding, unexcelled for assembling relatively heavy carbon-steel tubing, is not suitable to lighter and more expensive metals. While the bicycles pictured here were state-of-the-art for the curb-crunching days of yore, the 1980s were to be the decade of high performance.

company hit a new high with nearly 1.2 million bicycles sold, the company's heavy but indestructible ten speed counted for 325,000 of the company's total.

By this time, the greatest bicycle boom ever was in full force, triggered not just by fitness but by the environmental movement as well. (The first Earth Day was celebrated in 1970.) Still, something was missing. Despite huge numbers for the Varsity, Schwinn was not selling to a significant and expanding segment that had always represented the company's brick wall: adults. There was a report in the early 1970s, for example, that when a shipment of lightweight Raleighs arrived in Berkeley, California, young adults were grabbing and paying for them straight off the truck. Imports with strange names enjoyed runaway sales.

Schwinn dealers were selling all the bikes they could get at the time, but they also reminded marketing people in Chicago that they were getting the youngsters but not the parents. They told them to stop spending ad dollars on Captain Kangaroo. Do something that would get adults to buy Schwinns. The company heard the advice and in the early 1970s

1982 Fair Lady

1982 Lil' Chik

1982 Spitfire

they came out with the Suburban, with derailleur gears, a fat seat, upright handlebars, and a basket. By 1972, a good part of the Schwinn ad budget was going to *Reader's Digest*, which featured pictures of mature riders comfortably pedaling along on five- or ten-speed Suburbans.

Schwinn continued to be slow in producing a true racing bicycle, a style that was light and sleek and becoming almost unbelievably popular at the height of the boom. Then in 1973, Schwinn hit this market with a Japanese-built racer—its first foreign-made product ever—the Le Tour. Lug-framed and lighter than the classic flash-welded Schwinn, Le Tour was advertised in *Sports Illustrated* and got a quick surge in sales. Unfortunately, the bicycle boom was about to fall off almost as quickly as it started. In 1974, Schwinn sold 1.5 million bicycles; in 1975 they sold just

under 900,000. Le Tour just missed out on a market that had elevated names like Peugeot, Motobecane, and Cinelli to household-word status in many families all over America.

Schwinn continued to struggle with its image as the best bike for kids and the Sherman tank of the business, but efforts at fundamental change were mixed. Good, affordable racing Schwinns were being imported and a few of the authorized dealers were developing a legitimate adult market. But most Schwinns were still being bought for youngsters who were gravitating, for the time being, to a nameplate that they could pronounce.

Company sales were more than 900,000 bicycles in 1980—some 15 percent of the market. Results gave executives at Schwinn reason to feel good, but there were definitely storm clouds on the horizon.

Chapter Nine

TO THE SECOND CENTURY

$\mathcal{B}$y the late 1970s, the American bicycle was changing, though change was nothing new. Inventors and enthusiasts had been making improvements, sometimes fast and furious, for a century. What was different this time was that Schwinn had fallen behind.

Schwinn still sold Varsitys, Continentals, and other stalwarts of their line, and they were selling them by the truckload—more than a million bikes a year from 1977 through 1979. But this success was coming under the old rules, which meant a good, durable bicycle for children. And kids were no longer leading the industry. Adults were.

Ironically, Schwinn had sewn the seeds of the adult market itself—the very market that Frank W. had coveted for so long—when it made the Varsity an American staple. Adolescents learned the pleasures of riding distances on a Schwinn. Inevitably, they also learned that the pleasures were greater on the kind of bicycle that seemed distinctly un-Schwinn-like. That was lightweights which were truly light in weight. Lug-frame bicycles were becoming the rage, most imported with exotic French and Italian names. As ex-Varsity riders became college students, and as college students were transformed into young urban professionals, lighter and fancier foreign makes were purchased and ridden by people whose internal combustion vehicle of choice was a BMW.

Schwinn was selling lug-frame bicycles as well, primarily the Le Tour. But to get the public to believe in Schwinn as a light, high-performance machine meant changing its identity as the greatest kids' bike ever made. It wasn't that they didn't want to, rather they couldn't. Resistance to change rested partly in Schwinn's investment in flash-welding technology, absolutely first-rate for building bicycles of high-tensile steel but unsuited to anything lighter. With millions of dollars tied up in dies and machines to build Sting-Rays and Varsitys, Schwinn's flash-welding successes of the past made brazing bicycles of exotic metals a hard, slow corner to turn.

Going Places on the Air-Dyne

Schwinn developed new products in this period, though they sometimes came more by chance than by design. In 1979, they introduced the Air-Dyne Exerciser, which became such a success that it single-handedly enabled Schwinn to weather severe financial strains that the company faced in the middle 1980s. But it certainly came unexpectedly—one morning through the front door with a pair of product developers from Australia. The two Aussies worked for the research and development arm of Repco, that country's largest auto parts maker, and they were in the United States searching for someone to manufacture and market a recently invented "ergonomic" stationary bicycle.

Schwinn had been dabbling in exercise equipment for several years, but Executive Vice President Al Fritz believed that this one had exceptional potential. It achieved resistance through a paddlewheel of wide air vanes which

Left
The 1985 Tour of Texas, a stage race with stops at a number of cities throughout the state, was a major test for a Schwinn team that was having good success but was little-used in marketing the Paramount and a growing line of high-end racing bikes.

Above
In the late 80s, bicyclists were naturals for the box of a favorite breakfast cereal. Wheaties was a co-sponsor of the Schwinn team in 1988 and 1989. It was mostly road racers, but a sign that mountain-biking was here to stay was getting a few fat-tire racers in jerseys emblazoned with two very old names in the American marketplace.

from Australia—with pumping handlebars connected to pedals, it looked like a Rube Goldberg contraption.

Fritz naturally oversaw the Air-Dyne's redesign and then a credible marketing blitz. The result was that the exerciser became an astounding, if unlikely, success. They found a spokesman for it, not in the soft-spoken Captain Kangaroo, but in radio newsman Paul Harvey. Harvey liked the Air-Dyne—genuinely, it seemed—and wove it seamlessly into his news and commentary. The old radioman had some power over the cardiac set, and sales quickly grew to 50,000 Air-Dynes yearly and peaked at well over 100,000 in the late 1980s.

While a pitchman was crucial, the other part of selling Air-Dynes was another throwback—it was hustling, Schwinn-style. Just like old Ignaz in days gone by, no one could have been more enthusiastic than Fritz as he traveled the trade-show circuit. He was motivated partly by the fact that margins on Air-Dynes, which would rise in price to $700 at retail, were 50 percent while bicycle making was hardly breaking even at the time. But mostly it was the love of something completely new. At the bicycle shows, word got out that anyone going to the Schwinn booth "ought to wear a jockstrap" because Fritz was sure to get them on an exerciser and get them pedaling. It worked, and the Air-Dyne was an enormous money maker until 1990 when Schwinn lost a patent infringement case, an event that marked the beginning of the end of the family business.

Paramount Revival

It was a symptom of Schwinn's troubles in the 1970s that while Varsity sales remained high, Paramount

1978 Ergometric Exerciser. This was the second year for the ergometer which controlled resistance and regulated exercise. It was done with an automobile alternator "under the hood."

1979 Air-Dyne Exerciser. Australian inventors devised a system to maintain continuos workload with a paddlewheel of air vanes. Controls were mechanical, price was relatively low at $375 to start, and it all but replaced nearly every other excerciser on the market.

enabled the machine to perform the ergonomic aspect of exercise—regulating the amount of energy expended no matter how slow or fast the rider pushed the pedals. "Ergometers" of other designs were being used by heart patients at the time, but they were unwieldy. Schwinn's previous version used an automobile alternator as part of an electrical system to calibrate resistance.

Fritz encountered resistance of his own among his colleagues who doubted the Air-Dyne idea and especially the liberal royalty agreement he made with the Australians. Fritz argued that cardiologists were prescribing ergometers. The Chicago factory, moreover, was anxious to smooth out its production flow which was always slow in the winter. Still, skeptics in Chicago were fueled when they saw the prototype

declined. Paramount remained a superior racing-style bicycle, but in an era when the Italians were coming with some of the world's best new componentry along with an unbeatable image, anything American that had been around since the time of Emil Wastyn had a hard row to hoe. For reasons that had much to do with foreign fashions and less to do with racing mettle, Paramount was becoming an also-ran in the marketplace.

In 1979, Edward R. Schwinn, Jr., Frank W.'s grandson, was made president of the company, and one of his earliest decisions at the helm was to close down the Paramount operation until the model could be brought up to date. It was a fortuitous decision and opened the door for a new Schwinn engineer, Mark Muller, who took advantage of the opportunity and eventually became one of the best-known builders of custom racing bikes in the country.

Like so many other Schwinn employees, Muller began his romance with bicycles as a racer. In his teen years, he had respectable success on the road-racing circuit in and around Chicago, but as he got a little older he realized that the people he admired most, his real role models, were not the Fausto Coppis of the world but rather the Emil Wastyns. He took to designing frames and perfecting his brazing technique, and by the late 1970s he had a thriving cottage industry in bicycles for serious riders.

Muller naturally came to the attention of the ex-racers who populated the Schwinn organization, and Engineering Vice President Frank Brilando, the former Olympian, grew friendly with the young suburban kid who worked all week building frames and on Saturdays opened his small shop for customers. Brilando, looking

1982 Twinn Sport. Road racers met the bicycle built for two when Schwinn came out with the Twinn Sport in the late 1970s.

One of the Schwinn team's major events of the late 1980s was the Tour of the Americas, with stops beginning in Venezuela and ending in Florida. In 1989, Schwinn riders were among the leaders after various stages. Most were riding a Paramount with OS (oversized) tubing—thinner-walled than the chrome moly previously used, and marginally lighter.

Opposite
In 1982, Schwinn partnered with 7-11 stores and Eric Heiden to assemble one of the top teams on the American circuit. Here, a Schwinn racer rides the revived, state-of-the-art Paramount—at this point being built at a specialized Schwinn facility in Waterford, Wisconsin.

for a way to revive Schwinn's image, several times offered Muller a job at Schwinn. The youngster resisted until 1979 when one of his (he thought) better customers wrote a check for a pair of frames fully outfitted with premier (Italian-made) Campagnolo components. The check bounced for something like $3,000, whereupon Muller, then in his middle 20s, was ready to work for someone else.

For his first two years at Schwinn, Muller worked in areas that the company had been slow to develop—high-performance BMX, which former executives believed was too dangerous, and mountain bikes, which many old-timers found eccentric in the extreme. While Muller enjoyed some artistic success in these projects, Schwinn's hierarchy was focused on other problems besides new product categories. In 1981, for example, came the first of a series of tumultuous changes for the company—the announcement that the Chicago factory, beleaguered by labor strife, would close. Plans were for most domestic production to move to Greenville, Mississippi.

Quite separate from this move, however, was a scheme to reestablish the Paramount line in a small factory in Waterford, Wisconsin. This was Muller's opportunity: to run the Waterford operation and become, in effect, the guru of the bicycle that Schwinn hoped would rise to the top of the list for serious riders and racers. In many ways all of these things happened. Shortly after Muller took on the job, he embarked on a project to build nothing less than the ultimate custom bicycle of the prosperous 1980s. With a network of dealers taking orders, each Paramount would be built to the exact specifications of its individual rider. Everything was special-order, from the materials to the geometry and even to the paint. The concept instantly drew the interest of super-enthusiasts. Many Schwinn stores—at least those that kept pace with the lug-frame times—happily steered customers with $1,500 to spend to a factory that was in the United States and where everyone spoke English.

The Paramount concept naturally had a few kinks. Every true bicycle enthusiast, it turned out, was not a design genius, and Muller was getting drawings to build that looked more like Escher prints than bicycle designs. On paper, some angles and tube lengths might look buildable, but many simply did not work as bicycles. So for his first two years at Paramount, Muller spent hours on the phone with customers, telling one that the front wheel would hit the down tube, or another that the bike ordered would take more energy to steer than to pedal.

By 1983, Muller and product manager Dave Karneboge knew that the Paramount operation needed an adjustment. With the tacit support of executives in Chicago—by now embroiled in financial difficulties connected both to Greenville and off-shore manufacturing

In 1990, Schwinn was prototyping aluminum bicycles like the Ontare, shown here. The technology survived but not the name, which was challenged by another manufacturer.

1976 Scrambler. When Schwinn entered the BMX market seriously, the Scrambler had 20-inch cranks and 36-hole wheels, much like what San Fernando-area bike mechanic Russ Okawa was doing at the Canoga Cycling Center, a Schwinn dealership that was way ahead of the factory when it came to the next greatest thing in bicycles.

arrangements—they searched for a more standard formula for a custom bike. They settled on slightly oversized chrome moly tubing and determined a range of specifications from which customers could choose. Now Muller could spend less time explaining why a design was implausible and more time building bicycles that were.

Paramount became more productive. While numbers in the first two years neared 50 bicycles annually, they made close to 500 in 1983. Karneboge, himself a former racer who coveted Paramounts as a child, pushed the Paramount with particular enthusiasm. Sales competitions got good results, and leading the way was Helen's Cycles, a longtime Schwinn dealer in Santa Monica, California, which began selling more Paramounts and fewer of a high-end import that they ordered from Japan and marked with their own name. Another shop in Los Angeles sold Paramounts to several members of the Lakers—one with a 69-cm seat tube!

Perhaps the most impressive Paramount rider in the late 1980s was a Texas racer named Lance Armstrong. Armstrong, who had risen to the top in BMX competition, amused and frustrated Dallas-area bicycle dealers when he was a kid. "He always wanted something that we didn't have," said Jimmy Hoyt, whose Richardson Bike Mart was a mecca for serious cyclists in the 1980s. When Armstrong finally decided to concentrate on road racing, Hoyt talked him into a Paramount.

Whatever else this bicycle was, Armstrong decided, it was unique. He bought one and took it to his first U.S. Cycling Federation camp for juniors in Colorado. Within a couple of years he was one of the nation's, and the world's, top racers.

The Aluminum Edge

Some companies might have capitalized on Armstrong's success. But racing was not a big priority for Schwinn at the time. They had a team, started in 1982 with all the ambition of Ignaz Schwinn when he signed up Johnnie Johnson. For one year, it was headed by Olympic bicycle rider and skater Eric Heiden and was co-sponsored by the 7-11 convenience store chain. But when 7-11 decided to invest almost one million dollars in the program, Schwinn decided that amount was too rich for them.

Schwinn continued to field a team, but many people in the company wondered why. In fact, the undeniable prestige of world-class racers on Paramounts never did trickle down to the dealers who were selling slightly lesser models such as Super Sports and Pelotons. That would have required more advertising dollars than the company was prepared to spend. In fact, money was a big issue at the company in the middle 1980s because the new Greenville factory was consuming resources that had not been anticipated.

Whatever impulse Schwinn had to penetrate the market for high-end racing and touring bikes, they

SCHWINN

Schwinn Scrambler in action at the Encino, Calif. motocross track.

SCHWINN®

HIGH PERFORMANCE ACCESSORIES, TOO!

THE NEW SCRAMBLER™

THAT'S READY, BRAWNY AND BOLD!

Built to take it . . . strength and durability engineered inside and out! The Schwinn Scrambler frame is of heavy gauge steel tubing with extra brass fillet reinforcing at the bottom bar and cantilever stay . . . sigma steel reinforcing at the cantilever stay, seat mast and top bar. One-piece forged steel fork. Alloy front hub. Heat-treated cranks. Schwinn chrome plated tubular steel rims with heavy-duty .105 gauge spokes. Schwinn MX tires front and rear. Schwinn Hi-Performance style handlebar and cross brace. $122.95*

*Manufacturer's Suggested Retail Price, slightly higher in some areas. Prices and specifications subject to change without notice.

Black finish steel handlebars with a crossbar brace.

Pads and guards stems and frames. to fit crossbar

Extra padded Schwinn styled Schwinn Scrambler se

Black finish front hub assemblers.

Heavy duty black finished 20" cranks.

The Scrambler was advertised in 1976 in *Boy's Life* and in a tour that went around the country. The banana seat was not quite right for the track, however, and the company made adjustments in subsequent years.

1979 Scrambler 36-36. Even though mag wheels were popular for their undeniable good looks, the real racers knew that the lighter spoked wheel, particularly the stiffer 36-hole variety, provided the highest performance for the track. At $154.95 it was a little cheaper than its mag wheel counterpart that Schwinn was making that same year.

Schwinn's BMX Factory Team made national news, but many of the riders came from the old haunts around the Canoga Cycle Center in the San Fernando Valley. Kevin Jackson of Sylmar, California, rode for Schwinn for some three years in the late 1970s and later went on to do stunt work in Hollywood.

explored through technology and a trend that was already in progress: aluminum. The relatively new American manufacturer, Cannondale, was already experiencing good reviews and decent sales with expensive aluminum racing frames. While some designers wondered if aluminum really was superior to chrome moly, Schwinn engineers were soon conducting tests on oversized tubing stock developed by Alcoa. The theory was that a larger diameter tube permitted thinner walls, and that could save some fraction of weight in the frame. Schwinn named the aluminum tubing PDG for "Paramount Design Group," hoping some of that name would rub off.

Aluminum proved promising. By 1987, a racer on the Schwinn team named Alan McCormick rode an aluminum frame in spring warm-up races in Florida. The frame performed well and appeared to overcome usual complaints about aluminum, such as stiffness. McCormick's bike was painted yellow, called "the banana," and based on McCormick's early performance, it drew good notice from the bicycle press.

But by the time the Schwinn aluminum was introduced to the public, there were problems. Initially called the Avion, later the Ontare, both names were challenged by other makers with something similar. Ultimately, the models were branded with numbers such as the 754 and 564, inspired by birthdays of individuals working at the Schwinn office. Beyond identity snafus, production

problems existed in Greenville, normal in any major plant start-up, but they came at a time when Schwinn needed a success very badly.

BMX Zooms By

Another enormous opportunity that came and went for Schwinn began in the late 1960s. BMX, "bicycle moto-cross," emerged as the logical next step for Sting-Ray enthusiasts who modified their bikes, mostly with new seats and tires, to create truly dirt-worthy custom racers. Kids had been racing this way for years before the first organized event in recorded BMX history took place in Santa Monica in 1969. What followed would change the bicycle industry beyond recognition in a decade's time.

The people running Schwinn at the time looked anything but kindly on BMX at first. They knew what was going on; a popular motorcycle documentary entitled *On Any Sunday* was released in 1971 and opened with spectacular sequences of kids on bikes sliding against berms and flying over jumps. But when Schwinn's West Coast sales reps recommended

introducing a model for the bicycle moto-cross market, Frankie Schwinn ruled it out instantly. Liability was an obvious concern, he said, and there was also the Schwinn lifetime guarantee.

The chance to capture the BMX market was slipping by, though not everyone in the Schwinn "family" was ignoring it. In one of the hotbeds of early BMX, the San Fernando Valley north of Los Angeles, several tracks had sprung up, and organized racing took on a distinctly competitive tone. One bike shop that got deep in the craze was a Schwinn dealership, Canyon Cyclery in Woodland Hills, along with its nearby sister store, Canoga Park Cycle Center.

It started when a young mechanic at the Canyon and Canoga shops named Russ Okawa started customizing bikes, mostly Sting-Rays, with 36-spoke wheels and large flanged hubs that stood up to the punishment of

Above and Left
Schwinn weighed in at BMX tracks all over the country. In 1981, Schwinn banners and red racing suits were a sign that the company in Chicago was finally understanding that the action was at dirt tracks all over America.

141

The pros were not yet of driving age and some of the younger competitors in the 1981 National Bicycle Association Grand Nationals in St. Louis looked just big enough to see over their number plates.

1982 Predator. It looked good, it rode well, it had strong chrome-moly tubing and mag wheels. The only problem with this bike in 1982 was that it was not made by one of the growing number of BMX specialists in California. It would take time for the Predator to compete, if not on the track, then in the bike shops of America.

the track. Okawa's customers were soon the class of the San Fernando BMX circuit, and they never stopped looking for ways to improve their bikes.

Before long, the "Schwinn Team," as they called themselves, were even modifying frames—shortening the down tube, raising the bottom bracket, and increasing the clearance. This permitted a larger front sprocket and longer crank arms, the power advantages of which were quickly obvious. Okawa was not alone in making custom bikes. A number of garage mechanics in the area took to building and selling BMX frames, too—a few of whom would grow into major bicycle corporations in a decade's time.

Despite resistance in Chicago, Schwinn got involved in BMX more or less through the back door. It began after one of the garage mechanics, a former drag racer named Skip Hess, started buying parts from Okawa and later directly from the Schwinn warehouse. Hess was just then developing a line of BMX bikes that would later become the Mongoose Bicycle Company, and it was the beginning of what might have been a beautiful relationship. By the mid-70s, in fact, the Schwinn parts department was even handling Hess's Motomag wheel.

Eventually, Schwinn management softened its stand on BMX and started an official BMX "factory team" that toured the country, and it looked like the company was poised to lead this obvious growth segment of the industry. Okawa managed the team as they traveled from city to city, with local Schwinn dealerships organizing races where local kids could compete against the hot shots from California. Though the team left several Holiday Inns in less than pristine condition, the tour of 12-, 13-, and 14-year-olds was almost everything that the company could want. Then in 1976, Schwinn named its top rider, John George, as 15-year old spokesman to introduce the Schwinn Scrambler, a 20-inch frame outfitted much like Okawa had modified the old Sting-Rays.

Whatever hopes Schwinn had, however, were disappointed. The Scrambler was technologically run-of-the-mill. Meanwhile, salesmen from Mongoose and another small California maker, Diamond Back, were going to races, talking to kids, and getting their bikes into stores Schwinn held exclusively only a year or two before. In LaFayette, Louisiana, for example, Jay Wolff managed

Capital Schwinn and put a BMX track in next door. The store may have said Schwinn on the door, but the bikes kids wanted said something else, and as Wolff describes it, Schwinn's middle-aged salesmen never knew what hit them. Chrome moly, butted tubing and lighter 20-inch rims were available from a half-dozen other manufacturers, and Schwinn, America's bike for decades, was passé with a whole new generation of riders.

The Sting was Schwinn's attempt to recover in 1979. It was light and strong—Okawa and Mark Muller worked on the design. The whole thing was chrome plated, and components were serious, since the Schwinn parts department knew the BMX trade as well as anyone. It was too little too late, however. The once-small California makers that had started in their basements were now big names with the young kids who bought BMX bikes by the hundreds of thousands. Schwinn would remain behind the BMX curve for the next decade and a half.

Mountain "Klunkers"

If you wanted a pedigree in the next big trend in bicycles—the mother of all trends—you could not have

The 1982 Mag Scrambler had state-of-the-art geometry, mag wheels, and even a decent price tag for the BMX enthusiast, but a generation of cyclists had begun to turn away from the name that was once the most coveted in all bicycledom.

143

done better than to have the name Schwinn. The simple fact is that mountain bikes began as nothing less than a revival of the Schwinn balloon-tire cruisers of old. Nor was this bit of history forgotten. When mountain-bike pioneer Joe Breeze inducted Ignaz and Frank W. Schwinn posthumously into the Mountain Bike Hall of Fame in 1994, he declared simply and even solemnly: "They gave us our tire."

"Ballooners," as Breeze and other mountain bike pioneers called old Schwinns with 2 1/8-inch tires, were the bicycle of choice early on when kids with long hair took to trail riding around the landscape overlooking San Francisco Bay. Breeze, his old friend Gary Fisher, and other early mountain bikers began in the most low-tech fashion possible—pushing "klunkers" (another affectionate name) up steep slopes and racing down mountain trails of a mile or more.

Breeze and Fisher were long-time serious cyclists, members of Velo Club Tamalpais and training hard in and around Marin County, California, just north of the Golden Gate Bridge. Several were elite racers. Fisher was a top regional junior as a teenager, though there was

1982 Varsity. Two decades after it was introduced, the Varsity was still a mainstay of the Schwinn line, a great moneymaker but something of an image problem as lug-frame bikes from foreign makers were getting increasingly popular among the set that hankered after not a big motorcycle as in the days of yore but a BMW.

Right and Opposite
In 1984, freestyle was a big thing in BMX and the Schwinn Predator was strong, fine looking, and well-suited to some of the most impressive moves on a bicycle since the tricksters of Vaudeville had taken to bicycles decades before.

and several of his friends worked in bike shops, they found "antiques" of their own, fixed them up, and gradually fell in love with them. "It was the primitive side of cycling," said Breeze. They didn't abandon serious bicycles, at least for a while, but before long screaming down dirt roads occupied more of their time. By 1976, they even had a semi-formal race course on nearby Pine Mountain, the famous "Repack."

The bikes they used in those days are now museum pieces. One of Breeze's first klunkers was a 1937 Schwinn (apparently it began life with a B.F. Goodrich head tag) that he found in the back of a shop in Santa Cruz. Fisher found a 1937 Excelsior (a Schwinn brand) outside a barn in Redding, California, where the frame had been sitting for at least two decades and probably more. Fisher's housemate Charlie Kelly, another Club Tam member, had found the farm where countless old

1985 Bantam, Fair Lady, and Lil' Chik. High-tensile steel tubing and flash welding were still the hallmark of the Schwinn line in the 1980s. Its image was as a family bicycle company. (The Bantam was a "convertible" with a removable top tube.) They were good bikes and big sellers but did little to revamp Schwinn's image as a bicycle better for nostalgia than for a stimulating ride over the mountain and through the woods.

some difficulty with cycling authorities when he refused to get a haircut. In 1972, Breeze traveled to Europe for a cycling trip that was highlighted by a visit with Cino Cinelli. "I felt like I was shaking hands with God," he later said.

It was not God that lured the teenagers into the hills, nor even the landscape. It was the bikes. Club Tam members first took notice when older friends were riding old ballooners in the hills in the late 1960s. Since Breeze

frames had been discarded. "It was like plundering Rome," Kelly later said.

Fisher's reputation as the father of mountain biking may have come from the fact that he was the first to outfit an old Schwinn with relatively new parts such as longer cranks (prewar Schwinns had luxurious clearance), expander brakes, and a five-speed freewheel in back. This was hardly the makings of a new industry, but the races on Repack—named because coaster brakes burned oil on the hard course and needed to be repacked regularly—were getting more popular and more competitive all the time.

In 1977, these riders read an article in the serious counterculture periodical, *Co-Evolution Quarterly*. Mountain biking was being done in the Rocky Mountains, too, it said. The article was about firefighters in Crested Butte, Colorado, who rode old ballooners—they had been pedaling around town for a long time—over

nearby Pearl Pass to Aspen. The 40-mile ride was arduous, and when the Marin County group heard about it they decided they had to try it themselves.

In 1978, there were forest fires so the Crested Buttians were otherwise occupied, but the next year, they all met in Colorado for what is now remembered as the spiritual confirmation of the mountain bike movement. Already, Fisher and Kelly were making and selling bikes from a storefront near their homes. Joe Breeze had designed and built a model that featured many of the virtues if not the look, of his old Schwinn. In other places as well, a cottage industry was brewing, and Pearl Pass showed everyone that riding off-road was no local phenomenon.

Quite naturally, Schwinn employees in northern California were interested in these developments but didn't know precisely what to do about it. Regional manager Dave Staub stopped in on Fisher from time to time to discuss his frame designs, which were loosely based on the 1930s Schwinns. Staub wondered if steeper angles weren't better for riding on trails. Fisher and Kelly, then more focused on riding down hills than up them, preferred a more "relaxed" geometry. Meanwhile, Staub was having trouble making executives in Chicago understand what they were talking about at all.

If more evidence was needed, it came from Durango, Colorado, where a Schwinn dealership called The Outdoorsman was stretching Varsity frames to fit balloon tires, and locals were riding them on old hiking and motorcycle trails in the mountains above town. John Glover, manager of The Outdoorsman, remembered that it was low tech and low-performance, but converts were being made.

Fortunately, converts were also beginning to include Schwinn management, and their first mountain bike, the Sidewinder, was not too different from The Outdoorsman's customized Varsity. Sidewinders sold well enough, but again it was clear as early as 1980 that the mountain-bike industry was being driven by other makers. Specialized was bringing its Stumpjumper in from Japan by the containerload and quickly made it the bicycle of choice for riders in a completely new market; Schwinn responded with additional attempts at high performance. The King Sting was an oversized BMX-style Sting. The Schwinn parts division brought in some lugged mountain bike frames from Japan. But mostly, Schwinn was leaving the new market to others.

By 1984, the company came out with some higher-performance mountain bikes, including the High Sierra, also built in Asia. The High Sierra was well engineered—chrome moly, tig-welded, cantilever brakes. More significantly, a High Sierra was ridden by a racer who was winning races all over the West in the mid-1980s. That was Ned Overend, a former road racer, former triathlete, and former Outdoorsman employee. Overend was already in his late 20s when he became the leading mountain biker in the country.

Schwinn quickly agreed to sponsor Overend. To make sure that something came of it, they also sponsored the first National Off-Road Bicycle Association (NORBA) National Championships in Durango in 1986. Overend won easily that year and then won the next; women's-class champions those two years were on Schwinns as well. They were not stock Schwinns by this time, but rather Paramountains, made in Waterford by Mark Muller and quite probably unexcelled by anything on the mountain at the time.

For a moment, Schwinn had lurched forward to claim the legacy of Frank W. and the balloon-tire revival. But of course it was not that simple. With an enormous sales network to support, Schwinn raced but it never could put the effort into "guerrilla marketing" that smaller companies like Ross and Specialized could. Big signs at finish lines had other company's names. Romancing writers in the growing mountain-bike press was something that Schwinn never mastered. Simultaneously, the company was hemorrhaging cash due to several foreign manufacturing schemes. And the new Greenville plant had quality-control problems just when the mountain bike market, like the road bike market, was waiting to see what they had.

The company, in fact, was going bankrupt. It was a long road, but in retrospect, a certain one. It began when

In the mid-1970s, Gary Fisher was one of the pioneers of mountain biking when he found his circa 1937 Excelsior (an alternate brand name of a Schwinn #C97 Motorbike). He souped it up with heavy-duty expander brakes and racing gears and became one of the top competitors on the Repack race course in Marin County near San Francisco. He later developed his own line and has retained his reputation as one of the fathers of the mountain bike. Meanwhile his old klunker, partially restored, is a museum piece in the Mountain Bike Hall of Fame in Crested Butte, Colorado.

Schwinn transferred the majority of its production to the Taiwanese company, Giant Manufacturing Corporation, which by 1986 was producing 80 percent of the Schwinns on the market. This, by all accounts, was excessive dependence on any one supplier. Ed Schwinn attempted to diversify production with Greenville, with a stake in China Bicycles of Hong Kong, and several other facilities for niche products from Watsonville, California, to Budapest, Hungary.

The downfall of the family company owed to many factors. Ultimately, the timing of these moves was unfortunate. Production problems in Greenville collided with quality problems in Hungary, for example. Losses in these facilities were combined with competition of newer and more agile companies taking the clear lead, especially in mountain bikes, which represented an astonishing 70 percent of the bike market in the early 1990s.

Schwinn looked like a dinosaur, at least to creditors who were owed millions by the company. Then Schwinn lost its Air-Dyne patent-infringement suit, and in 1990 "the bankers' sirens went off," wrote the weekly

1982 King Sting. By 1981, Schwinn was adapting the engineering for its high-end BMX bike, the Sting, to the burgeoning mountain bike market. The result was the King Sting.

1983 Cruiser. The idea of mountain bikes was already changing America's taste for cycling comfort when Schwinn took advantage of the fat-tire movement and introduced its retro Cruiser with balloon tires, cantilever frame, padded seat, and basic paint.

Opposite
1982 Sidewinder. While old Schwinns are credited with being the original mountain bikes, the company's first intentional mountain bike was actually a Varsity frame outfitted for fat tires. It was a logical solution but a low-tech one that quickly yielded to the lighter metals, better geometry, and superior componentry of a whole phalanx of competition—like Specialized and Ross—based in California.

Stepped up from Schwinn's first mountain bike, the Sidewinder, the Sierra boasted durability—which meant heavy-duty flush welding—and several high-end features like aluminum-alloy rims and cantilever brakes.

Opposite
Not all mountain-bike events were held in the mountains. In 1984, a race in Chicago's Lincoln Park had Schwinn team member (and later manager) Mike Ferrell sprinting across a grassy straightway.

Crain's Chicago Business, which covered Schwinn's bankruptcy in a number of detailed articles. The company was anything but extinct, but it was going to take a new set of owners and managers to make Schwinn anything like the force it had once been in the American bicycle industry.

Rebirth at 98

The renaissance of Schwinn Cycling & Fitness, as the company was rechristened, began in 1993 when the family business was sold to an outside investment group. The partnership relocated the company from its ancestral home in Chicago to a place where mountain bikes were not just a business but a passion, Boulder, Colorado. It was a sad, even devastating, chapter in the annals of a legendary American industry. Yet the bike trade, and especially longtime Schwinn dealers, hoped that the new company might get closer to the techno-

logical changes that were transforming bicycles with unbelievable speed.

Schwinn's new owners, a Boulder-based ski-equipment maker called Scott Sports Group, backed by maverick Chicago investor Sam Zell, had little patience for the old. Thus, the former Schwinn line was nearly erased and replaced within three years—an almost amazing feat—by a small team of designers. There was something passionate about this group, which included Skip Hess, Jr., whose father was the founder of Mongoose, and other graduate engineers who were also expert mountain bike racers.

"Legendary innovation" became the slogan of equally ambitious marketing people. The phrase referred to the unmatched legacy of Ignaz and Frank W. Schwinn. New Schwinn's objective was not too different from what Ignaz did in the 1890s and what Frank W. did in the 1930s. That was to place the engineering and mar-

The 1995 Black Phantom was the result of enormous research and tooling to reproduce in exacting detail the bicycle that had filled the imagination of America's youth nearly two generations before. Now, of course, it was to cost something like $3,000, but regaining a piece of childhood was never meant to be inexpensive.

keting functions of the business in almost transcendental harmony. It was helped by the fact that Schwinn's new managers were as young and hungry as the founders of any small start-up company.

By 1995, the Schwinn Homegrown line became their signature, with aluminum frame, race-worthy geometry, and prices from $1,200 to $3,000. Remarkably, it took the company only two years to design and produce eight high-tech models with features well beyond what the average rider needed. But in bicycles, for better or for worse, image really was everything, and Schwinn was building a new image.

In mountain bikes, it meant delivering something completely different in a new rear-suspension system. For a design, Schwinn quickly tapped a

patent by an MIT-trained bike enthusiast named John Castellano. Bicycles were not the only things that inventor/entrepreneur Castellano did, but they were definitely his favorite. Since 1987 he had worked on projects ranging from a frictionless tone arm (which never reached production before CDs made the idea obsolete) to a trail-capable wheelchair that he produced and sold himself.

Ever since he was a kid in New Jersey, Castellano had worked on bicycles. When he was 15, he even fit pieces of old bikes together and built something similar to a "swing arm," the basic mechanism that he finally developed for rear suspension. Later when he moved to southern California to take a job with Hughes Aircraft (to work on the Space Shuttle) he designed features for

his own mountain bike in his spare time. For hard trails, the concept of suspension continued to fascinate him, and in 1992 he finally worked out what became the "unified rear triangle," also known as the "isolated drivetrain." It took him a while to file for his patent, but even before he did he went to bike shows where he got the engineering staff at Schwinn to take an interest in his design.

It might have fallen through the cracks; the company was about to change hands. But late the next year, his Sweet Spot patent was applied for, and he sent his prototype to Colorado. Extensive testing and further prototyping followed, and Schwinn's conclusion was that Castellano was right. The precise position of single pivot, the "sweet spot," was critical for a

soft ride when the rider was seated and a stiffer ride when standing or cranking. As Schwinn engineer Mark Schroeder tested and refined the concept, Schwinn put it into production for 1995.

It was a new way to do business for a big bike company. But in a way, Homegrown mountain bikes were also a tribute to the 100-year-old Schwinn legacy. The whole project was not unlike something that the Schwinn family might have done in decades past—the point is that they did their best work when times seemed hardest. Calling it hard times at this point seemed like an understatement. Yet they pushed innovation and even put their faith in an unknown bicycle designer in California.

Perhaps the Schwinn name was blessed, for good things began to happen. The Sweet Spot was "endorsed"

Team Schwinn in 1995 was poised for a comeback in mountain-bike racing. Tammy Jacques and Brian Foster were among professionals riding Homegrowns and joining many Americans in training for the ultimate proof that mountain biking had arrived: the 1996 Summer Olympics in Atlanta.

1996 Homegrown Factory XT
Homegrowns are at the top of the Schwinn line, made in Durango, Colorado, at a plant owned and operated by Schwinn. Whatever it takes to get back on top—that is the new Schwinn's attitude. In this case it takes a price tag of $2,500, reasonable by today's high-end mountain bike standards.

with a bit of negative advertising from the competition. Even initial production problems at a factory in Seattle came with a silver lining: Schwinn quickly purchased the Yeti Mountain Bike Company in Durango, and Homegrowns were built successfully by an "in-house" factory in their second year.

While one part of the market was impressed with the latest in mountain bikes, another had something else in mind: cruisers. Vintage-style balloon-tire bicycles had more appeal than ever, along with old cars, Humphrey Bogart movies, and anything else that reminded people of a simpler time. It did not hurt with the slightly older set that 1950s-era Schwinns, especially Black Phantoms, were just about the most comfortable bicycles ever built.

Engineers at the new Schwinn embarked on a "Cruiser program" shortly after taking over the company. In fact, retro-styled bikes called Cruisers had been built and sold by Schwinn for more than a decade, though they were unimpressive. They used mountain bike forks, which lowered production costs but raised the front end—intolerable to someone who remembered how the ballooners of old responded around turns. Stems were different, too, as was the bend radius in the cantilever struts. Transferring production from Chicago to Taiwan had taken its toll; moving cantilever-bike production to Hungary in the mid-1980s "cannibalized" it even worse.

Now, the new Schwinn's managers were determined to restore some of the old luster. They began by sifting through a dusty cellar in Chicago shortly after the company was sold. Great design was one of old Schwinn's past strengths, and what the engineers found was a treasure trove of drawings, and particularly plans for one of the best balloon-tire bicycles ever made, the 1955 Black Phantom.

In late 1994, Schwinn's new Cruisers were introduced. They were entirely up-to-date technologically, with chrome-moly frames, hollow forks, and aluminum rims, but they had unmistakable vintage proportions. Not only did the line share the handsome profile of the old, they had the sense of balance and rideability that made the Black Phantom so superior in its day. The result was an instant artistic success; within months Cruisers were a commercial one as well. "We wanted to prove to the old dealers that we new guys had a sense of the past," said one of the engineers. They succeeded.

In 1995, as if to prove it again, new Schwinn next came out with not just a Cruiser but perhaps the ultimate Cruiser: a "commemorative" 1955 Black Phantom produced as part of the company's centennial celebration. Engineers in Colorado reproduced the '55 with absolute fidelity, each part recreated from new tooling. Some pieces were easy, like the kickstand. Others were almost preposterous, such as a lower fork crown with

1996 Homegrown (full suspension). The "unified rear triangle" and "sweet spot" for the pivot are designed for the most efficient ride possible—stiff when you're standing and soft when you're sitting. The competition is taking pot shots at the theory behind it, so Schwinn engineers must be doing something right.

Cycelock. The solution in the case of the latter was to cast it by lost-wax process, more familiar to artists than to manufacturers. It was one of the most painstaking bicycles ever produced, and one of the more expensive that year at $3,000 per copy.

Cruisers alone were not going to restore Schwinn to financial health—mountain bikes and hybrids remained the clear leaders in bike volume in the mid-1990s. But new balloon-tire models certainly restored the battered company's image. Cruisers and the Phantom were just about the most distinctive things in bike stores in 1995.

The retro-bike movement made an immediate impact—imitated but not equaled by others. "People made the historic connection with these bikes. They came from a more comfortable age," said Dennis Hostetler, a second-generation Schwinn dealer at Glen Ellyn Schwinn in Illinois. Cruisers sold by the hundreds at Hostetler's shop, which also sold three commemorative Phantoms for the full $3,000 as soon as they came in.

The executives of Schwinn Cycling & Fitness hardly had time to pause. When they caught their breath they admitted that there really was something to selling a bicycle with one of the most famous names in America. More than that, there was something else in being Schwinn. It meant having a tradition. It inspired good engineering. It encouraged risk taking. Most of all, Schwinn history taught that nothing succeeded in the bicycle business like a pure love of bicycles, a quality which kept the family in the business over more than a few rough spots.

By the mid-1990s, another bicycle boom was well under way, though people who peered ahead came up with more questions than answers. Who would pay more than $3,000 for a bicycle and why? Had bicycle technology run its course? Some sought new directions for the industry.

In any case, old-fashioned values such as loyalty to dealers and customers and hard-headed idealism seemed like the best road map anyone in the industry could find. It made the heirs of Arnold, Schwinn & Company look past their 100th birthday and talk optimistically about the company's second century.

Competitive mountain biking once meant the thrill of downhill racing. As the technology improved, and riders toughened, pedaling up the mountains became as big a deal as screaming down them. Here, Team Schwinn's Mike Kloser demonstrates.

INDEX